IF ONLY HE HAD DIED

IN THE WAR

The Impact of Suicide on Surviving Family Members

By SHIRLEY AVRAMI

Cover picture - **Shirley Avrami**

To Gideon, Sharon, Yuval and Alon. For Everything

CONTENTS

FOREWORD...7

INTRODUCTION 9

THE PHENOMENON OF SUICIDE 12

    Adam[1] 22

SOCIAL ATTITUDES TOWARD SUICIDE....................................... 25

    Rachel and George 28

SUICIDE SURVIVORS 34

    Hannah and Nicole 36

GRIEVING PROCESS 46

FEELINGS TOWARDS THE DECEASED 50

    Susan 53

PREOCCUPATION WITH RE ASONS FOR THE SUICIDE 57

BEREAVED SONS AND DAUGHTERS..59

    Leonora 68

MEN AND WOMEN: SUICIDE AND GENDER DIFFERENCES 75

    David 78

    Meryl 80

A DATE WITH DESTINY? 85

    Marsha..87

FEARS AND COPING 91

    Joe 94

PARENTAL ROLES...96

    Ron 99

    Maya 103

---

1   All names have been changed to ensure anonymity.

SPOUSAL SUICIDE.. 107

    Joel 110

    Nancy...113

BEREAVED PARENTS.. 120

    Tracy... 123

    Naomi 126

    Sandra 134

SUICIDE OF A SIBLING... 139

    Mark 142

    Kevin... 148

I WISH HE HAD DIED IN A WAR: THE HIERARCHY OF BEREAVEMENT ..151

    Saul... 154

    Roz.. 156

DEATH WITH DIGNITY... 160

    Michelle 162

    Sheila 165

EPILOGUE 170

ACKNOWLEDGMENTS.. 173

BIBLIOGRAPHY 175

FOREWORD

Prof. Albert C. Cain

Department of Psychology

University of Michigan

I have earlier had the privilege of reading Dr. Avrami's thesis, 'The impact of parental suicide on the surviving children', and her related writing on survivors of suicide. I was therefore already assured of the value of this book.

The mental health field in general, and suicidologists in particular, have long focused on the suicidal individual him/herself, whether the studies were on sociodemographic variables, such as age, race, gender, religion, rural vs. urban settings, marital status, pre-existing psychopathological syndromes, such as major depression, schizophrenia, bipolar disorder, alcoholism; preceding and/or precipitating events, such as hopelessness, despair, self-loathing, shame; suicide methods such as firearms, barbiturate poisoning, hanging, jumping and more recently, biochemistry and genes.

Surely this accent on the suicidal individual is warranted – yet for a long period it was to the virtual exclusion of any attention to the impact of suicide upon those left behind. Of course family, but also friends and others who had significant relationships with the deceased as well. Yet, as an early director, H.L.P Resnick, of the US National Institute of Mental Health's center for Studies of Suicide Prevention satirically stated the case in an editorial "The neglected search for the *Suicidococcus Contagiosa*" that "...this pathogen is found dormant in the psyches of those who have lived with anyone who has killed himself." He then contrasts the lack of public health attention to this pathogen versus that of "... the *gonococcus*, a much less lethal pathogen than the *suicidococus*."

Recent decades have witnessed a modest but increasing recognition of the plight of suicide's survivors, expressed both in escalating systematic empirical research and services (typically support groups), with the primary focus on surviving spouses, and secondarily on parents of adolescent suicides.

This book enriches our suicide survivor literature, and thankfully does so not by a misguided attempt to measure, for instance, what percentage of some grossly selected convenient sample of suicide-bereaved widows reveal a DSM-IV disorder six and eighteen months post-loss. Rather it provides a richly textured, multidimensional, qualitative picture of suicide survivor reaction, not jammed into artificial categories. It provides the overlapping but distinctive perspective of survivor spouses, survivor parents, survivor children, and survivor siblings, in a manner that permits such contexts to illuminate each other. It permits the survivors to speak relatively fully in their own voices rather than check boxes, circle rating scale numbers, or select from a set of multiple choice responses to pre-determined questions. It does so with the enlightened disclosure and emotional honesty more likely to be elicited by an interviewer who is openly self-identified as being a participant in the community of survivors. It does so from a community of volunteer samples rather than one with the built-in bias of patient samples.

And finally, it sensitively depicts this often transformative experience of suicide survivors with full respect for their anguish, their resilience, and ultimately their individuality in a manner that moves them out of the shadows of secrecy and stigma.

INTRODUCTION

Dr. Shirley Avrami

I was almost nine years old when my father committed suicide. I vaguely recall my grandmothers whispering to each other "He is no longer..." and little me, not really understanding that if he is "no longer...(here)", then where is he? I do remember understanding, although perhaps only in retrospect, that my father had disappeared from my life.

Not only was my father 'gone' as my grandmothers said, but it was obvious to me, even though no one told me directly, that he had vanished in a terrible way and that to talk about or remember him was taboo. It became clear to me almost immediately that just as he had disappeared from our lives, so too, stories about him, reminiscences and references to the person he had been, were now gone. This person was now no longer part of our lives. From observing the way others around me behaved I quickly learned not to speak of him. In a way I didn't really miss him. I did not know who to miss.

No one came to talk to me or explain anything about my father's death, not how he died, nor why. The fact that he committed suicide was revealed to me by chance, even though part of me had known all along. Since he was never mentioned at home, it was clear that something about his death was mysterious. I suspected there was something to hide, although I did not know what.

Throughout the years at major crossroads in my life, when I wished him with me, I tried to feel his presence by conjuring up vague memories. It was at times such as my matriculation exams, my wedding, and the birth of my children, that I felt his absence acutely. The stark reality for me was that at the age of nine he simply vanished.

I don't remember the moment of truth as being one of relief. I had no one to share this moment with, and I still didn't feel that from now on I could speak about him or share memories of him, and obviously I could not refer to the way he died. The revelation of the suicide did not change anything for me. The suicide had been such a secret, yet the facts remained unchanged.

It was always hidden – 'what would happen if they found out'. I was afraid that if people found out that my father had committed suicide, they would think badly of *me* – not of him! It was only much later when I realized that there was a stigma attached to those whose family members committed suicide and I understood that I was not alone with these feelings and fears, and in the patterns of behavior I had developed for coping with these emotions.

It took 25 years from the day of his death until I was able to talk about him. It was then, when I was finally able to talk about him with courage and face the question of how he died, that I finally succeeded in saying the word 'suicide' without it sticking in my throat. Suddenly I could not understand why I had hidden the details of his death for all those years.

Why was I ashamed of someone else's actions, which had occurred when I was a mere child and in which I played no direct part? It was clear to me that this was no way to function. When asked how my father died or where he was, I should not have cringed inside. I should not have felt that lump of unshed tears, sticking in my throat.

When I was younger I was unfamiliar with the term 'support group', but as an adult I thought I might find answers among people who had had similar experiences to mine. I set out to find other people whose parents had committed suicide. I wanted to talk to them and find out how, if at all, this had affected their lives. I wanted to learn from their stories.

Based on my own experience, my initial research focused on stories of people whose parents had committed suicide. When I conducted the interviews it became clear to me that the experience of each and every person who has had a relative commit suicide is unique. When I spoke of the research I was frequently questioned as to why I was interested in this subject at all.

I could almost see the wheels spinning in the minds of the interviewees and other people who heard of my research, as doors opened into what had previously been locked away, blurred or obliterated. As I began to speak to people, stories emerged, the story of a grandfather who had committed suicide but who was never spoken of at home, an uncle whose story was veiled in secrecy and whose suicide was never referred to.

As a result of these conversations I decided to publish these stories.

I felt that writing a book and making the stories public would enable me to bring the topic of suicide out of the dark.

The meetings I had with people whose relatives had committed suicide were captivating but at the same time daunting and frightening. Each meeting had me riverted back to parts of my own story, helping me to confront my own experience which, until then, I had repressed. Each and every story added another dimension, an additional layer of experience. This, in turn, increased the understanding of the ordeal experienced by a relative of someone who had committed suicide.

When the research was published I received a flood of letters from parents, brothers, sisters, widows, and widowers, of those who had committed suicide. I discovered that there were many people who were dealing with the pain, the stigma, the secrecy, the guilt feelings, and the shame associated with the suicide of a relative, and with the effects of these emotions on the family. I met grieving parents, children, siblings, and partners of those who had committed suicide. Many of these people were attempting to deal with feelings of guilt and responsibility for the tragedy, and at the same time had to continue with their lives and attempt to rebuild their family from the time prior to the suicide.

I hope that the interviews presented below, together with local and international publications on the subject, will shed light on the varying responses to suicide, and on the effects of suicide on the different individual family members. This, in turn, will provide a unique insight into these families.

THE PHENOMENON OF SUICIDE

This book focuses on the impact of suicide on the surviving family members. Questions concerning the ways in which this impact manifests itself, how long does the impact last, and the dilemmas and fears faced by families, are all addressed. How, if at all, can this impact be minimized. How can the individual family members cope with the painful fact that one of their relatives has committed suicide. And how can they still lead full, productive lives.

This book is based on interviews with people who have lost a relative to suicide. The interviewees repeatedly spoke of the difficulty of revealing their story to others, and if they did speak about it, felt the need for a particularly close relationship with the listener. Among many of the aspects of suicide addressed in this book is the question of what happens with feelings that have been hidden for years. It examines where they are channeled, and discusses the price survivors pay for suppressing these feelings.

But first, one must look at the act of suicide itself. Who commits suicide? Do these people have common psychological, social, or physiological characteristics? In a particular situation why does one person commit suicide while another person does not? This chapter introduces a discussion of the phenomenon of suicide and draws on the perspectives of sociologists, philosophers, and artists.

The writings of poets who committed suicide, while lyrical and poetic, may still reveal feelings of agony, anguish, and a world of terror and suffering. When we speak of poets who committed suicide, the beauty of the words is inextricably bound with the tragic ending of their lives.

In his book *Beyond Guilt and Atonement*[1] the philosopher Jean Amery, an Auschwitz survivor, discussed the question of the limits of human

---

1   Jean Amery, Beyond Guilt and Atonement. Tel Aviv, Am Oved 2000

capacity to face unbearable conditions such as torture, and the diverse range of possible responses. He said that life is fragile and may be ended voluntarily at any minute, yet there is always what he called 'the hope principle'. Amery took his own life in 1987.

Until recently the subject of suicide was taboo, and discussion of it was avoided. In the 1950's Nissan Turov wrote of suicide as "... a subject which requires extra care, because although there is a wealth of information concerning it, it is still shrouded in obscurity; we actually know very little... and there is also the fear that discussion of it is dangerous, perhaps it is better not to talk about it at all."[2]

Today the word *suicide* is heard more often than in the past. It is less common for people to whisper that someone who committed suicide 'died under tragic circumstances'. Nowadays society even considers some acts of suicide, such as committing suicide due to a terminal illness, to be more legitimate than others.

Recent data has shown that almost one million people worldwide commit suicide each year and the suicide rate amongst men is four times higher than amongst women.[3]

Irit Gutter, an educational consultant on adolescence, published an informational booklet for parents in an attempt to increase awareness and therefore prevent suicide amongst adolescents.[4] She claims that one must look for possible signs of distress in the poetry and songs that adolescents write. She mentions the book *In the Name of All Pain* published after the suicide of the author, Ron Adler, at the age of 19.[5]

> "And then
> After I wrote
> After I cried
> I died."

Nathan Yonatan, another poet, in his opening remarks in Adler's book writes about the two faces of suicide: "One stands in awe and fear in the face of the deed of a 19 year old young man... What despair was in this personal decision, full of loneliness and pain – to leave this life."

---

2   Nissan Turov, The Problems of Suicide Tel Aviv, Dvir, 1955
3   NIH 2011
4   Irit Gutter, *Suicide Amongst Adolescents and Families Bereavement*. Jerusalem, Hebrew University 2004
5   Ron Adler. In The Name Of All Pain. Tel Aviv, Sifriyat Poalim, 1979.

Al Alvarez, in his book *The Savage God: a Study of Suicide,* discusses the different aspects of suicide. He compares the Middle Ages, when it was acceptable to connect art and melancholy, with the following era which connected genius, creativity, and early death. He quotes Honoré de Balzac who presented the dilemma he thought authors faced: "To kill feelings and live through to old age or to accept a saintly death and die young –– this is our destiny."[6] Alvarez notes that at that time most young artists were immature in their treatment of death and saw it not as the end of it all, but as the ultimate dramatic gesture directed against a boring, bourgeois world. Suicide was considered *romantic* and these artists felt that this *suicide as a gesture* would create a situation in which their personality would survive even if the body died.

Alvarez also claims that those who committed suicide believed that they themselves would somehow witness the drama created by their suicide. In 19th century Europe, poetry, youth, and agony, became synonymous. Many poets committed suicide at an early age. Their perception was that life itself would corrupt them, thus they felt they would find redemption in life after death. In fact, some of these poets did become legends. It is worth mentioning here however that adolescents tend to express themselves dramatically. Not every piece of dramatic poetry or prose about death, or every discussion of death by adolescents should be cause for concern. Adolescence is the period in life when preoccupation with philosophical questions about life and death is not uncommon.

Suicide is probably the only situation in which a person looks death right in the eye, yet even people who feel that they are totally in control of their lives and believe they can plan every aspect of their lives do not generally feel that they can also plan their own death. Today when people are constantly being challenged and presented with new ideas, suicide is still perceived as threatening, dark, and something which has the potential to become an epidemic. This phenomenon of suicide as an epidemic seems to be the justification for not discussing suicide openly. To a certain extent, this is reflected in the way in which cancer was referred to, as the disease, rather than by its name, as if the very mention of the word cancer increases the chances of getting it. Sometimes when I (the author) tell intelligent, open minded people that my father committed suicide I can see the emergence of the irrational attitude through their behavior and body language.

---

6   Al Alvarez. *The Savage God: a study of suicide.* W. W. Norton & Company, 2011.

There is no doubt that both the concept and the act of suicide are threatening. Suicide makes us confront our own mortality, something that most of us spend our lives trying to avoid. The idea of death is frightening and the thought that a person has chosen to bring about his own death raises philosophical, theological, psychological, and ethical questions. It is in this context that various writers speak of the complex way in which humans treat death; with the utmost confidence knowing that they will eventually die but their absolute inability to imagine it happening. They cannot visualize themselves as lifeless.

Albert Camus opened his book *The Sisyphus Myth* with the words: "There is only one serious philosophical problem: Suicide."[7] In deciding whether it is worth living this life or not, one is answering the fundamental question of philosophy. He explained that the importance and depth of the suicide question arises from the rare link in philosophy between the theory and the deed arising from it; hence this is a question which involves a high degree of responsibility. What makes one philosophical question more important than another hinges upon the resulting acts.

Camus referred to suicide as a phenomenon which takes place in the world of the individual. He saw it as a personal rather than a social issue. He also talked about the trigger which he saw as the incident which transforms a thought into an act. He spoke of many reasons to commit suicide but added that ultimately, one cannot know for sure what triggered it.

Camus made the connection between suicide and the most fundamental question of all, the question of the meaning of life. One continues with the daily routine of life, mainly out of habit. When a person takes their own life they are saying that this habit, this daily mundane existence lacks meaning or purpose. Ultimately, Camus did not consider suicide as an appropriate solution to the meaning of life. He felt that the meaning of life comes from within.

In his essay *An Absurd Reasoning*, Camus wrote about death, referring again to the meaning of life. Initially the question asked was whether life needs meaning in order to live it. He indicated that the opposite appears to be true and that it would be better with no meaning at all and with no role to fill. For this reason Camus saw Sisyphus as a happy rather than a tortured person (As punishment for his evil deeds, Sisyphus was condemned to purgatory where he had to roll a boulder up a hill to the mountain peak only to have the

---

7   Albert Camus, *The Myth of Sisyphus*. Tel Aviv: Am Oved, 1979. Translated from French by Zvi Arad

rock roll back down the mountain. He was condemned to do this for eternity). Sisyphus knows that this is his destiny but gives it meaning, seeing the very struggle to reach the peak as fulfilling. This supports Camus' claim that we must imagine a happy Sisyphus.

In his book *Man's Search for Meaning*,[8] Viktor Frankl, an Auschwitz survivor, wrote that even while coping with the most difficult situations, finding a reason to live and looking for the meaning of life was a better alternative than suicide. Frankl wrote, "Even in Europe in the sixth winter of the Second World War our situation was not the worst that one could imagine... "...one must find meaning in one's own life, even in what seems a hopeless situation. One must have faith in the future."

The ability of another Auschwitz survivor, Jean Amery, to cope with torture was also derived from his ability to perceive torture as relatively tolerable. In his *Essay on Torture*, written in 1965, he said that "what was done to me in that cellar was far from the worst of all experiences; it did not even leave visible scars."[9]

Another approach towards suicide is presented in Plato's *Apologia*,[10] where Socrates speaks of death as a preferred alternative to life without self-respect. He talks at length about his attitude towards death and the fact that it is a punishment only to those who fear it: "I did not think that because of the risk I should not act as a free person and I do not regret it; for it is much better to die after having defended myself like this, than to live with such behavior... the difficulty is not so much to escape death; the real difficulty is to escape from doing wrong. Death is one of two things. It is either annihilation where the dead have no consciousness of anything, or it is really a change – a migration of the soul from this place to another. And if death is indeed a kind of sleep without feeling, there is an advantage in dying."

The definition of suicide varies according to the perspective of the particular discipline from which one examines it. Most experts agree that bringing about one's own death is an act of self-destruction. Edwin Shneidman,[11] a pioneer researcher of suicide, noted that the main characteristic of suicide is a step taken in order to reach a solution to an unresolved crisis with which a person is unable to cope. The purpose of the act is to stop the

---

8   Viktor Frankl, *Man's Search for Meaning*. Tel Aviv: Dvir 1981. Translated By HaimIsack

9   Jean Amery, *Essay on Torture* Tel Aviv: Am Oved, 2004 translated from German by Yonatan Nirad

10 Plato, *Plato's Writings*, Tel Aviv: Schoken publishers, 1997, Translated by Joseph Libes

11 Edwin S. Shneidman, On the Nature of Suicide. San Francisco, Jossey-Bass 1969

conscious flow; the main trigger is unbearable psychological pain and the one committing suicide wishes to terminate that feeling of pain. People commit suicide when their psychological, rather than physical needs, are not met. The main feeling that leads to suicide is helplessness. People planning to commit suicide feel that no one and nothing can help them alleviate the pain or resolve the situation they find themselves in. People in distress approach suicide in a somewhat ambivalent manner, both planning the suicide and yet looking for ways to find help. Prior to committing suicide these people generally go through a process of narrowing down the opportunities they feel are available to them to solve their problems; their cognitive situation is one of escape – trying to alter the situation in which they find themselves. Shneidman noted that their way of life is characterized by self-hostility and an inability to enjoy themselves and the world around them. Their inner world is full of turmoil and confusion from which they cannot escape. Their way of thinking is agitated and they dichotomize everything they face into bad/good, black/white, therefore every day existential questions, lead them to dead-end feelings, resulting in the search for a way to die manifested in suicide attempts or suicide.

Israel Orbach[12] noted that suicide is not a question of fear or courage, but a way of overcoming unbearable psychological pain which cannot be ameliorated. He quoted Heinz Kuhot's theory of the self, where the person eliminates the self in order to erase a reality that is filled with disappointment and feelings of failure, in order to preserve one's self, even if the price is death. Orbach[13] also noted that for the one contemplating suicide, death is perceived as a tool to satisfy needs, based upon primary trauma and biological, or even genetic, factors.

According to psychoanalytical theory, suicide is an expression of a complex process after the loss of a significant other, due to death, separation, or neglect. Identification with this figure prevents the possibility of directing anger towards the deceased and this anger is replaced by self-punishment. Thus in suicide, the power of self-destruction takes over one's soul. Normal development is a process in which the child separates psychologically from his parents. According to this approach, suicide represents an inability to separate from one's parent figures. Hence a threat of separation may lead to suicide, paradoxically, in order to remain tied to the loved one forever. This

---

12 Israel Orbach, *Children Who Don't Want To Live*. Ramat Gan, Bar Ilan University. 1987

13 Israel Orbach (2001). Epilogue. In: Al Alvarez: *The Savage God: a Study of Suicide.* Jerusalem: Carmel.

occurs particularly with people lacking love and confidence.

The pioneering sociological research into suicide was that of Emil Durkheim.[14] He claimed that by committing suicide people kill themselves fully understanding what they are doing. He named four links between society and its members which he saw as explanations for suicide. The first presents values, norms and society's expectations of their fulfillment by the individual. These norms lead to suicide as a sacrifice, for example hara-kiri in Japan. Durkheim defined this kind of suicide as *altruistic*.

The second link between individuals and society exists when the latter does not take care of its members. This reality may cause a sense of loneliness and people who lack social support networks such as family, community, and so forth may see suicide as a solution. Durkheim called this *egoistic* suicide.

The third type is called *anomic* suicide. This arises as an outcome of a sudden crisis in one's life, such as losing social status, losing one's job which in turn leads to financial loss or other life crises.

The final type which Durkheim discusses takes place where there is highly regulated social and environmental control. In these situations individuals might feel that their freedom is curtailed and in order to regain this freedom they choose suicide. Durkheim named this suicide as *fatalistic*.

In his book *The Writer and Suicide* [15] Boris Akunin talks about the link between suicide and the arts. He says that every person who lives not only through his body but also through his soul, sooner or later considers the possibility of suicide; for a creative person this possibility is more likely to arise than for the others. Sometimes the reader may find the connection through the way in which the author presents suicide. In this context Akunin mentions the phrase *literaturcide*, suicide in literature. This was first mentioned by Arthur Rimbaud.

When talking about writing which may lead to suicide, Goethe's *The Sorrows of Young Verther*[16] is most commonly mentioned. The hero of this short story has become a model to youngsters around the world, and major or even minor disappointments have led them to follow his example. Klages, in his book *Goethe als Seelenforscher* called it Vertherian fever. It is worth mentioning in this context that Goethe himself in response to the critique

---

14 Emile Durkheim, *Suicide – A Study in Sociology*. Illinois: Free Press 1951

15 Boris Akunin, *The Writer and suicide*. The author wishes to thank the translator Yigal Liverant for letting her use his translation from Russian.

16 Goethe, *The Sorrows of Young Verther*. Tel Aviv, Sifriyat Poalim 1980.

said that his writing did not cause but rather exposed the evil in these young souls. In most cases talking about suicide is a means of overcoming the fear of death and not surrendering to it.

In his book *A Tale of Love and Darkness*[17] the well-known Israeli author Amos Oz writes about the impact of his mother's suicide on his own life. He talks about the feelings of abandonment, his anger, and at the same time his own feelings of guilt towards her.

In her book *The Suicide Index*, Joan Wickersham[18] ended her story about her father's suicide by commenting, "I know I will never know the whole story. I will never feel his death in the full, direct manner I would have liked to feel it; and, at the same time, I will never stop feeling it."

The first connection between art and suicide is obviously with Van-Gogh, but other painters, such as Modigliani, also committed suicide. Alvarez wrote at length about the connection between suicide and the arts, especially painting. He said the 20th century was characterized by more radical, violent art than the previous centuries, containing numerous symbols of self-destruction. The primary example, as he put it, was the DADA stream which presented a violent approach towards everything, not only to the establishment but also to the arts. According to him it was characterized by violence, shock, black humor, and suicide, all outcomes of World War I.

In the introduction to the book *Letters to Anthon Van Raffard*,[19] Van Gogh's death is graphically described. Van Gogh's letters afford us a glance into his world of sorrow. Although in the first letter, dated September 12th 1881, Van Rafard tried to convince his friend not to succumb, he later spoke of the physical attributes of painters as being characterized by "... sudden weakness, nervousness, and melancholy."

The question as to whether or not suicide has underlying physiological attributes is a complex one with both threatening and comforting aspects. In the future it may perhaps be perceived as any other disease, without the mysterious aura that surrounds it today. This aura both mystifies it, and at the same time confuses the researcher trying to study it.

It is somewhat comforting to think that future medical research may be able to explore the physiological and biological causes of suicide (if

---

17   Amos Oz, A tale of Love and Darkness ,Jerusalem, Ketter Publishers 2002
18   Joan Wickersham, The Suicide Index: Putting My Father's Death in Order. Tel Aviv, Achuzat Bayit 2011. Translated by Dana Elazar-Halevi
19   Vincent Van Gogh, *Letters to Anthon Van Rafard,* Translation and Introduction (Hebrew) G. Talpir. Gazith Press, 1944

indeed there are any) and in this way predict populations at risk and aid in prevention. At the same time it may also mean that there is a shred of truth in the myth that there are "... families in which *they* commit suicide", as Adam (one of the interviewees) said. These families may need to be more aware than others, of signs of distress within the family.

Findings from several studies have strengthened speculation of a biological-physiological aspect of suicide, yet at the same time there are some scholars who claim that these findings are preliminary and controversial. Zalsman et al[20] noted that suicide does indeed run in families, and is partially influenced by genetics. A connection was also found between suicidal behavior, aggression, and impulsivity. The American researcher Carol Ezzell[21] claims that post mortem brain surgeries revealed differences in the brains of people who committed suicide and those who died of other causes. Suicide is not necessarily connected to depression, but to other psychological and physiological patterns. In other words it is seen as a disease which may exist with or without the presence of depression or schizophrenia.

Mann et al[22] noted in their study that relatives of people who committed suicide were found to be at higher risk for developing mental disturbances than people in a control group where there were no relatives with a history of suicide. They suggested that some kind of malfunction in the serotonin absorption mechanisms and other cerebral factors in the hypothalamus may be predictive for at least some suicides. Complex biological tests have identified serotonin as a main neurotransmitter which has to do with depression as well as with suicidal behavior.

A meta-analysis carried out by Hawton et al[23] found that the main risk factors connected to suicide were prior suicide attempts and feelings of hopelessness. The factors which were tied to suicidal behavior, and not necessarily to an actual suicide, were a family history of suicide and severe mental disturbances. Other research carried out recently, has revealed a model in which the predictors of suicide are life events, biological factors

20 Zalsman, G., Frisch.,Apter, A. and Weizman, A. (2002). Genetics of suicidal behavior: candidate association genetic approach. *Israeli Journal of Psychiatry and Related Sciences* 39(4) 252-261

21 Carol Ezzell, C. (2003). The neuroscience of suicide. *Scientific American*

22 Mann, J.J., Currier., Stanley, B., Oquendo, M. A., Amsel, L. V. and Ellis S. P. (2005). Can biological tests assist prediction of suicide in mood disorders? *Journal of Neuropsychopharmacology* (21)1-10.

23 Hawton, K., Sutton, L., Haw, C., Sinclair, J. and Harris, L. (2005). Suicide and attempted suicide in bipolar disorders: a systematic review of risk factors. *Journal of Clinical Psychiatry* 66(6): 693-704.

such as disturbances in the serotonin and norepinephrine activity, and at the same time depression and impulsivity.[24] Brent et al[25] also noted that suicide and suicidal behavior is highly familial, and transmission of suicidal behavior is partly attributable to genetic factors. It appears to be transmitted independent of familial transition of psychiatric disorders per se.

Research in this area is still in its early stages. The difficulties derived from the complexity of this phenomenon are as with some other phenomena, that this exists only in the human race. In his book *Suicide and the Writer*, mentioned above, Akunin says that a major difference between man and animals is that man is aware of his own death, and this allows him to choose whether to live or die. He quotes Sartre who also noted that one of the differences between man and animals is that man can kill himself.

In her book *Night Falls Fast: Understanding Suicide*,[26] Kay Redfield Jamison argues that the perception that suicide is unique to mankind carries the assumption that suicide is rational. This in not necessarily true and one may make a partial comparison, between suicide and self-destruction which does exist among some animals.

Is suicide a problem which lies in the body or in the soul? The truth is that it probably lies somewhere in between.

In some cases at least, the tendency to commit suicide is indeed a disease like many others where the pathology is not yet known or understood. At the same time, one may presume that if someone does have the physiological propensity for suicide, an emotionally sensitive situation is also needed for the suicidal tendency to be realized.

The perception of suicide as a physiological disease may alter the way suicide is studied and researched in the future, and may therefore lead to increased financing of medical research in this area. This could mean that, like other illnesses which were surrounded by an aura of mystery only because their cause was not yet discovered, so too suicide may be transformed from a mysterious, frightening phenomenon to an illness like any other. As such, it is expected that in the future its cure will be found and a change in social

attitudes will take place. These will be discussed further on.

---

24 Suicidality and Data Collection – Workshop Summary, 2010. Washington DC: National Academic Press.

25 Brent, D. A. and Melhem, N. (2008). Familial transition of suicidal behavior. *Psychiatric Clinics of North America* (31)2, 157-177

26 Kay Redfield Jamison, *Night Falls Fast: Understanding Suicide.* New York: Knopf 1999

Adam

I am twenty two. My father committed suicide about ten years ago. When I was growing up I thought everything was perfect, but there were secrets in our house, things I knew nothing about.

We had a big house, cars and were not lacking for anything. I didn't realize that something was wrong until it was too late. It happened when I was twelve. He was a really decent, honest, man but financial problems in his business were too much for him and he couldn't cope.

We were making a bonfire, and he went off to bring some more wood. I waited and waited by the fire, but he never came back. After a while I went home and saw all the neighbors gathered around. There were already rumors flying that something had happened to him. Only two weeks later was I told the truth about how he really died. I heard people talking about what had happened, and there were all sorts of stories surrounding his death.

For me he was everything, my father, my friend, and a father-figure to all of my friends. At first friends helped us but as the years went by, they vanished. It was as if I was to blame, as if it happened because of me. I saw this happen not only to me, but also to my mother with her friends. People think that suicide is a kind of epidemic. Society does not know how to cope with death in general, and especially not with suicide. I don't know what they thought. Maybe they thought that we were crazy. People started gossiping. We lived in a small rural community at the time, but finally it reached the point when we felt we couldn't stay there any longer so we moved to the city.

Clearly his suicide had an impact on my life. From an economic and social point of view, the situation at home had changed completely. In addition to all the emotional pain, we also lost our home. For me, as a child, it was very sad to celebrate my Bar-Mitzvah like this. People told me that I was now the man of the house, but when I tried to take on this role, it was problematic... I found it very hard to accept the fact that this had happened. I also changed. I was no longer a good little boy. It took many years before I was myself again. I supported my mother throughout the years, but my friends deserted me.

My father's suicide totally changed my life, and one of the ways in which it hurt me the most was that I completely lost my trust in people. My father trusted people – and it killed him. I suspected everyone even though I hadn't been like this before.

My father liked to travel. We used to go hiking every weekend. And he did *it* out in the country, out in nature which was the place he loved most. He shot himself and left us a letter... a letter which explained nothing.

(Interviewer): You sound angry....

Of course I am! I understand that he had problems, but this isn't the way to solve them. Money isn't everything! He took loans from friends and couldn't pay them back. He couldn't look them in the eye. But I think that sometimes you have to swallow your pride; so yes, I am angry because he left me, my two little brothers, and my mother, without a father and a husband. Killing yourself isn't a solution. What about us, didn't you think about us? Just like that, leaving us with all the problems? How am I supposed to grow up normally, to mature, when the house needs a man? Being a father is a unique role. I had no one to learn from. So I feel more anger than empathy (towards my father)...lots of anger. Suicide is not the solution, when you have a loving wife and three kids.

I became very tough and introverted. I blamed the whole world, and didn't want to accept help from anyone. Today I am different; I look forward to the future; but I know that what my father did will affect me for the rest of my life. I think about it constantly...not a day goes by without me thinking about it. I think that other people who go through some kind of crisis think that perhaps they too are capable of doing it. If he did it, why won't we? But one must understand that suicide is not the solution. What is money? You have a family, friends... why not look at the positive things in your life?!

From time to time the question of why he did it comes up. As a child I couldn't understand many things, and obviously I couldn't prevent the tragedy, but when I was asked how my father died, I found it difficult to reply. There is such a taboo surrounding suicide, and people are so judgmental when it comes to talking about suicide, so when I was asked about him, I tried to ignore the question and avoided answering. When I did reply and told people that he had committed suicide, they would back away and leave me, sometimes even in the middle of the conversation, just like that! Even now, as an adult, every time I have to answer the question, "How did he die?" the person who asks the question ultimately does not know how to react to the answer. When people hear it was a suicide, they think this is that kind of family in which *they* commit suicide. ***They*** – do you understand? I think this explains why our friends deserted us, and it's humiliating. I think it would have been better for us had he been murdered. It is difficult to talk about it with people who aren't in the same boat, not on the same wavelength. I used to say that he died in a car accident, or I changed the subject. Yes, it also would have been better had he died in a war.

Sometimes I wonder what I'll do when I have kids; how will I tell my children about their grandfather? People don't talk with kids about these things; kids are naïve and might tell their friends.

He was everything to me, and for me... everything. So when he disappeared and I needed a father, I didn't have one. I saw my mother in need of help. Today I have 'man to man talks' with my girlfriend's father, talks about things I can't discuss with my mother. I didn't have a father to look up to, to learn from.

Yes, it's true, when you see your mother involved with someone else, it hurts. A kid has only one father. Today I can understand her, but at the time – people talked about her, and that was tough for me. In the letter he left us he wrote that he loves us, and added something that I now see was unfair to my mother – "don't cheat on me." When I was a little boy I used to remind her that this was his last request. I guarded her like a watchdog. Instead of living my life I lived hers. I felt that I had to take care of her. Often I thought that maybe what we were told wasn't the truth. Maybe someone threatened him, forced him to take his own life. To this day, his own sister is unwilling to accept that he committed suicide.

When I start talking about it I feel better. I hope that one day people will stop judging me. Why should I feel guilty about something my father did? But sometimes I feel that perhaps I could have prevented his suicide, and I didn't.

I wasn't sure whether I should tell my girlfriend about the circumstances of my father's death, because I knew from experience that there are people who abandon you once they hear the story. In fact I didn't tell her the story until she confronted me saying that she didn't think I was telling her the whole truth about my father. After I told her I asked her not to tell other people.

I feel that a person who commits suicide either doesn't think about the implications, or perhaps they think too much. One always wishes for the best for their loved ones and strives to shield them from pain and suffering. I think the most important thing is that children, whose parents have committed suicide, should get help so they don't have to find their own way alone, like I had to.

SOCIAL ATTITUDES TOWARD SUICIDE

The punishment that society imposes on a member who breaks the unwritten rule that one should not choose one's own death is that of stigmatizing the person who has committed suicide, and also the people associated with that person. This punishment is for carrying out a forbidden, unacceptable act. It appears that the power of stigma is not as great today, and the act of suicide is considered less a part of a hidden, forbidden, world than in the past. There is one aspect of suicide however, about which little is known – the surviving family members. What happens to the family of the person who committed suicide? What impact does it have on their lives? Is there anyone at all to support them, to help them in their mourning and grief? Is their mourning process similar to that of someone whose relative died some other way? It appears that for the surviving family, the stigma and taboo still exist, and these are not part of the changes in attitude toward suicide itself.

After the suicide, the family is tainted. The whole family becomes 'a family in which *they* commit suicide'. The relatives suffer both from the loss, and from the social price they have to pay for the manner in which their loved one died.

One thing I heard expressed over and over in the interviews for this book was the feeling that society judges the survivors harshly because of their relative's suicide, whether it was a parent or parents, a spouse, a sibling or a child. One of the saddest statements I heard in this context was from a mother whose son committed suicide when he was a teenager "... if only they would stop looking at me as if I am a monster..." The harsh judgment and condemnation of the relatives reflect the fear of suicide itself. The categorization of causes of death into 'legitimate' and 'non-legitimate' are based on circumstances which society accepts, and those it does not. It sees the 'non-legitimate' cause as a source of shame for both the deceased and the family, and creates a hierarchical ladder according to the degree of honor or disgrace the death brings to the family, relatives, and close friends, the *suicide survivors*.

Over the years social attitudes towards suicide have changed. Ancient Greek philosophers perceived it as a legitimate solution to existential problems. Christianity changed it completely, and suicide was forbidden by law. The Council of Arles declared suicide a crime in the year 452 BC, and in Prague, in 563, suicide was condemned and penalized by denial of proper burial rites. In addition to these, there was also civil punishment and confiscation of family property. Only after the French revolution in 1789 were these laws repealed. Until the end of the 19th century in the United States, people were sent to jail after a suicide attempt.

Orthodox Judaism sees life as a gift of God, belonging to God, and not to mankind. Thus suicide is perceived as murder. In most cases however, there is an attempt to ease the pain of survivors with the claim that the one who committed suicide was not sane at that particular moment and therefore that person will not be denied life after death, which is deemed to be the most important reward for a believer. According to Encyclopedia Judaica, the sanctity of life and the obligation of a person to preserve his own life are central to Judaism. It is customary amongst Jewish people, and not only very religious ones, to bury those who have committed suicide in an isolated part of the cemetery or even outside the boundary of the cemetery.

While the suicide itself might not cause the family shame and humiliation, the negative reaction of society to suicide results in creating feelings of shame. Since social disapproval cannot be directed at the person who died, the criticism and the negative allusions are directed at the surviving relatives, thus creating a stigma. The easiest way for the family to avoid being labeled and stigmatized is to conceal the circumstances and manner of the death as much as possible. In most cases not just the cause of death, but any discussion of the deceased, is shrouded in secrecy. Consequently, the entire existence of the person is concealed, suppressed and eliminated from the family story. Stigma and secrecy become a central part of the survivors' experience. The dictionary defines stigma as a sign of disgrace which in turn results in feelings of shame and humiliation on the part of the family which is now 'labeled'. While not obviously visible it is very perceptible.

As much as possible the family returns to its regular routine after the suicide but the person who committed suicide is often never mentioned again, as if they never existed. This occurs sometimes when the family internalizes the hidden, nonverbal messages they receive from society implicating the family and holding it responsible for the death; sometimes there are verbal messages which lead to the same end result —the relative who committed suicide is erased from the family's narrative.

Rachel and George

Lisa, Rachel and George's daughter committed suicide when she was 22 years old.

Rachel: Lisa was... she had everything anyone could ask for. She was gifted, talented, clean, tidy, everything a mother could want. She started studying at university but after seven weeks she said it was too difficult for her. I told her to take a break, get away, relax and then go back to her studies. But she said it was really difficult, that she couldn't sleep and that she was barely eating. She was depressed, both physically and mentally depleted. She asked for help and a date had been set for her to begin therapy on campus... but she didn't go. She decided to come home instead.

One day when Lisa was sleeping over at a friend's place, at about six o'clock in the morning her friend called saying that Lisa was threatening to kill herself. I couldn't believe it, I thought it was nonsense. We didn't understand what she was talking about.

Nevertheless, my husband went right over to bring her home and when she came in she seemed like a different person. She was very quiet. I prepared things she loved to eat, but she had no appetite. I asked her, "Lisa, what's going on with you, why do you want to do this?" to which she replied, "I just can't go on this way."

We took her to a psychiatrist who gave her some pills but these didn't help. She also started meeting with a psychologist. During one of their meetings the psychologist called me and told me to come and get Lisa immediately. Lisa always drove by herself to their meetings, but on that particular day the psychologist said that Lisa could not possibly drive home by herself. When I arrived the psychologist told me that Lisa had threatened to commit suicide. She had taken George's pistol but couldn't manage to fire it. After that there was a period of about a month in which she cried a lot and she didn't eat. Her friends came to take her out. They went to various different places. Lisa suddenly developed a love for jazz.

We took a vacation, in order to spend time with her. We also didn't want to leave her alone. We thought that all this would pass after a short period, and then she would go back to university. But she wouldn't hear of it.

George: She didn't want to hear the word 'University'. She demanded that we bring all her belongings back home.

Rachel: She would lie here, putting her head in my lap.

George: ... like a four year old child.

Rachel: She kept saying to me "Mum, I'm scared..." I told her "You have your whole life ahead of you, what are you afraid of?" I didn't understand the extent of her suffering. Afterwards we learnt that her anguish was so severe, it was impossible to understand. She wanted to sleep in my bed and she kept asking me to hug and kiss her. She wanted to be close to me. Then she decided to get a job. She began working in a shop where she had worked before she began studying. Then, one afternoon before she was leaving for work I called her just before she was about to leave home. She left for work and... she didn't come back. That's it.

George: That morning she had an appointment with her psychologist. After the meeting the psychologist decided to follow Lisa and later he told us that he had seen her sitting at the bus stop writing something. We assume that it was the letter she left for us. She came home, ate lunch with her brother, took the dog out for a walk, and then headed off to work but she never got there. We don't know if she deliberately went to the tower because she knew the place, or whether she went there on impulse, without any previous plan. Whatever it was... she jumped from the tower.

Rachel: We received a phone call from the police saying that something had happened to our daughter. When we reached the place we were told she had jumped.

We have two other children, boys. She was not very close with the elder one, but actually in the previous few months she had been helping him with his homework in Math and Physics because she was really good at these subjects. He was fifteen and a half. At first he felt very angry towards her... and you know what... so did we! We gave her everything possible, never said no to anything she asked for. She studied electronics and had all the equipment she needed. It was very expensive but we made every effort to buy it. She was even awarded two scholarships.

George: Only thirty students out of a thousand were accepted to study Architecture. She was accepted to other universities but only wanted to go to a particular one.

Rachel: After the army she went to work, saved money, and then travelled in the Far East for half a year. Then she began her studies. Her grades were always high and every year we were told that she was an outstanding student.

We miss her so much, all the time. Next January it will be nine years since her death. Seven months after she died I started writing to her. I felt I wanted to talk to her, to tell her about, and share both the happy and the sad occasions in the family. I also shared what was happening politically. I write to her every week or two. She chose the 'perfect time' to do it. George was due to go away for a few days, and she did it before he left.

She would often say, "I feel like I'm sinking!" Then there were days she would say, "I feel like I can see the light." I was so pleased and would encourage her, hoping that she would relax a little more.

George: In the month she was back here from university she wanted to work, and a friend helped her find a job. I was for the idea, but the psychologist was totally against it. "Why are you sending her to work, what if she doesn't make it?" He didn't want to let Lisa go to work. On another occasion Lisa went to sleep over at a friend's house, and came home beaming. The therapist reprimanded me again for going against his advice. I told him how happy Lisa looked when she came back. She looked like a new person.

(Rachel takes out the suicide letter wrapped in plastic.)

In her letter Lisa asked her parents, friends, and brothers to forgive her, and I (the interviewer) received permission to quote the following sentence from Lisa's letter, "May God forgive me for usurping His authority to terminate life", and it goes on to say "May you, my family, be strong for me in my weakness."

(I tell Rachel and George that this sentence in particular struck me since some people are angry with those who commit suicide because they dare to take on God's role).

Rachel: I thought this too. There was a kid in our street who committed suicide and I thought of what he had done to his family, what a fool he was... but we don't really know what they feel. We don't understand how unbearable the suffering is. It is not like having a pain in one's hand. Then you can take care of the pain. It is very difficult to soothe pain in the soul. In her letter she thought about everything, mentioned everyone and even asked us to donate her organs.

George: When she did it, she climbed up onto the roof of that building. There was another guy there. He asked her what she was looking for up there because the upper floors of the building were deserted. She said nothing. We later found out that he was waiting there for his boss. They both saw her jump.

Rachel: She was so gifted in every way and in everything she did. She made a party for our silver wedding anniversary. She arranged everything with the neighbors so that we would be totally surprised. And at that party she said (we have it taped on video) that she hoped we would all celebrate our 50th anniversary together, too. But no...

She was a girl who liked adventure, she hiked and travelled everywhere, she even went on a big trip to the Far East. You wouldn't have known that there was anything wrong with her. Until it started... maybe she didn't want to disappoint us, to let us down and perhaps she didn't want to disappoint herself. A grade of 90 wasn't good enough for her... and at university perhaps she didn't do as well as she'd expected, maybe she lost confidence in herself. I don't know what she thought. She would constantly tell me that she was scared... I would tell her, "You are young, what are you afraid of? You are so young... so, you don't have to go to university." I figured she'd take a year off and return to her studies.

George: But she demanded a refund from the university.

Rachel: And then the guilt feelings started. Maybe we didn't take care of her well enough, didn't do everything to save her? The doctor said we should have her hospitalized but I couldn't bear the thought of hospitalizing our beautiful, talented girl. So we left her at home. Everyone came to see her; the house was full of her friends. After she did it I found a box full of letters she kept in her closet. The letters were from all her girlfriends who were always asking for her assistance, for her advice, and she helped them. She helped everyone else but she couldn't help herself.

I gave away a lot of her stuff, but I also kept quite a bit – her clothes, her perfumes... maybe if I needed her room I'd give everything away but this way I just keep it like this. I simply can't let go.

We had so many questions but there were no answers. And now we kind of go on, there is no other choice. We go out to the country, occasionally we even laugh, we meet with friends, but it's really only a facade. Obviously we go and visit her grave regularly, we clean it, put flowers there, arrange memorial services... and we have so many memories even though in her letter she asked us not to dwell on memories of her, but how can we not...

Our son is getting married next month. It's a bitter-sweet occasion, happiness mixed with sadness. When I write to her I tell her what a pity it is that you are not here with us, and with your brothers. One is getting married, the other one has just been released from the army. The whole time he was in, I prayed that nothing would happen to him. Obviously on the festivals when the whole family gets together it's very difficult for us.

I don't know if I have told you all there is to say. The longing for her, missing her is what it's all about. Just this week there have been a couple of suicides. They were reported in the press. People talk about it for a couple of days and then they return to their daily routine. What annoys me is the stigma. In general suicide is not understood. No one seems to understand the reasons why people commit suicide. Even our friends treat us differently. It's not the same as when someone dies in a war or in a terrorist attack. Then it's different. We have been labeled as the family whose daughter committed suicide, and the insinuations are that something must be wrong with us, maybe we did something wrong. We have been attending a support group of parents whose children committed suicide. Here we have heard that all these children were clever, beautiful, and from 'good families'. Perhaps within the 'good families' these children needed less personal inner strength. Ultimately it seems that these youngsters had a lot in common.

Someone in the group said that we, parents, have the right to live. This sentence struck a chord in me because for a long time after Lisa's death if someone would tell me a joke I wouldn't let myself laugh. I felt that I was betraying her. Participation in the support group has really helped me to cope by realizing that I'm alone and that there are others like me. I have so many memories, not a single day goes by when we don't think of her. I keep asking why, why, why, but I can't find any answers. There is no point even trying to explain it to other people, who keep asking me why she did it. How can I answer questions to which we, too, have no answers?

George: Look at her photo album, her childhood, high-school prom, weekend family visits when she was in the army, her trek to the Far East, and all the photos which show her love of nature, of landscapes, of people she met on her travels, and pictures of herself looking pretty, happy, laughing, and surrounded by friends.

Rachel: Here, look, when she was at school her friends made her a surprise party at home, and here is her brother when he was a little boy. You couldn't tell that there was anything wrong with her. She was always in a good mood. Here, look, with the kids in the family, she loved everybody. I so much looked forward to her wedding day, and to the day we'd have grandchildren. I see her girlfriends who got married, and have children, and I think to myself where would she be now, how many kids would she have had by now. It hurts. Well, I hope her brothers make up for it.

(Interviewer) What is their part in this story?

George: They don't talk. They don't ever mention her.

Rachel: Even if I start a conversation about her, they don't react. They don't react at all.

Many times I thought that maybe the big trek in the Far East had some kind of an influence on what happened. Perhaps returning home after all that freedom and going straight into the pressures of the university was too stressful. Maybe, but who knows. When we hear stories about other children who committed suicide, we have much more understanding of their families since it happened to us. Only someone who has gone through this and who has experienced a terrible loss like ours can understand the depth of our pain and grief. And there are many stories like ours.

At first when people saw me they would often cross over to the other side of the street. When someone asked how I was, I used to reply that everything was fine. I knew that if I told the truth no one would want to talk to me, people didn't know how to relate to me anymore. This is how I felt. People respect you if someone in your family died after an illness, or fell in the army, or in a terrorist attack for example.

It is so hard to understand what she did because she was so full of zest for life. She was such a good girl. She never fought with us even when she was a teenager. I used to tell George that he spoiled her, but it was impossible to say no to her. She was so good.

Since it happened, we don't sleep well. We wake in the middle of night; we think and think… one can't escape it. We live this nightmare twenty four hours a day and it will be like that till the end of our lives. I am sure it is like this for all parents who have lost their children. It's as if part of your body has been amputated, that's really what it's like. I keep asking myself, where did we go wrong, not only in the last year, but throughout her whole life? It eats me alive.

During the Shiva I barely shed a tear. I was so angry. I thought that there are people who cope with terrible diseases, with much worst situations than this, why did she have to do it? But afterwards I started to understand, and when I understood, I related to her depression as an illness. People, society in general, just don't understand this phenomenon. They don't understand that it can actually happen in any family.

SUICIDE SURVIVORS

I n his book "Survivors of Suicide"[27] Professor Albert Cain, who is considered as one of the "founding fathers" in the field of suicide survivor research, defined suicide survivors as people who were close to the person who committed suicide. These survivors could include relatives, friends, colleagues, teachers, physicians, in fact anyone who had feelings towards the deceased. He claimed that surviving families suffer from values, restrictions, and stigma, stemming from a society where suicide has a pall of guilt attached to it, a society which does not offer mechanisms to help survivors cope with their difficulties thus leaving them isolated with their grief. He said that the impact of the event on survivors may include denial, lying about circumstances of the death, feelings of guilt and anger towards the deceased, and yet may also include identification with the deceased, depression, search for meaning of the suicide, and an incomplete mourning process.

Edwin Shneidman,[28] another pioneer in this field of research, said in 1969, that for each suicide, there are at least five to six relatives who are affected by the impact of the suicide. According to this assumption, in that year there were 300,000 suicide survivors in the United States alone. He also found that relatives are left with a multitude of feelings, many of them negative, towards the deceased, and that these continue to exist, as a 'psychological skeleton', in the lives of the survivors.

Society deals with death and the deceased in different ways, according to the death circumstances. Research which compared attitudes towards people who have committed suicide, to attitudes towards people who died from other causes, found that not only were the people who committed suicide perceived as suffering from mental problems, but their families were also perceived as having mental problems, and as needing more assistance

---

27 Cain, A. C., (1972). Survivors of suicide. Illinois: Charles C. Thomas
28 Shneidman, E. S. (1982). Voice of Death. New York: Harper and Row

to cope with the death, compared to other families. This difference was found even when no other biographical details apart from the suicide were presented.

Research conducted in the United States[29] compared the grieving process following suicide, to grieving following a car accident or a heart attack for instance. Relatives of people who committed suicide were often perceived as having had the ability to prevent the suicide. Herein lies the guilt: not only the guilt felt by the survivors themselves, but the fact that in many cases society blames them, either overtly or covertly, verbally or nonverbally, indicating that not only did they fail to prevent the suicide, but even worse, in some way their behavior may have contributed to, or caused, it. In brief, suicide survivors are prone to internalize the negative attitudes of society towards the suicide act itself.

Many survivors with whom I spoke while writing this book were strongly affected by this negative attitude following the suicide. They felt stigmatized and labeled as 'a family in which someone had committed suicide'. For example Rachel pointed out that people crossed the street so they could avoid meeting her.

In his book *Suicide: the Ultimate Rejection?*, Colin Pritchard[30] claims that the family of those who have committed suicide becomes an invisible victim because society in many cases tends to blame the family for not preventing the suicide. He adds that a predominant emotion felt by these families is rejection – both from the deceased, and from society; that the deceased did not love his family enough to remain alive for them, and hence the suicide sends a message of rejection, and society also sends a message of rejection through its criticism. Pritchard further claims that by victimizing the family, the community (including professionals and therapists) relinquishes responsibility for not identifying signs of the impending suicide, thus denying its own sense of guilt.

What became clear from the interviews, was the feeling that when society labels individuals, they find themselves assigned involuntarily to a group in which the common denominator is not a simple one. This common denominator, in fact, creates an immediate bond between people who have lost a loved one to suicide. Expressions I heard repeatedly from my interviewees were 'brothers in arms' or 'blood brothers'.

---

29   Allen, B. et al (1993) The effect of cause of death on responses to the bereaved: suicide compared to accident and natural causes. *Omega* (28)39-48.
30   Pritchard, C. (1995). Suicide: the Ultimate Rejection? New York: Open University Press

Hannah and Nicole

Nicole: I was very excited to read of your research in the paper. Of course I could relate to it and it was important for me to meet you. It wasn't as if I hadn't spoken of the incident since it happened, when I was eight years old (I am forty one now). I first talked about it fifteen years ago but I have never met anyone else who had the same experience and this is what excited me. I really wanted to talk with you. So, are you interviewing me in order to include my interview in your book? Would you like to talk to my mother too? I'll ask her.

Hannah (the mother joins the conversation): I'll tell you whatever I can.

Nicole: It is always difficult to start. Okay, I had a father...whom I felt close to for eight years. I remember him as being very happy. For me the word 'music' is synonymous with the word 'father'. I am sure that my love of music comes from my mother too. We had a very musical home, also filled with culture, art, philosophy, and poetry. It's clear that my love for music came from my home. Recently I began to think that my involvement with music helped preserve my connection to my father. Music filled my soul; when I played the piano I always tried to do my best, to excel, and when I applied to the music academy, I simply *had* to be accepted. Not being accepted would have been a catastrophe. It was like a thread that linked us. I inherited these musical traits from him. He was a true artist, but he didn't make a living from his art. The influence of his music on my life connects us. Through it, he is always present.

Sadly, I hardly experienced having a father because a week before my eighth birthday, it happened. In our family it is referred to as 'the incident' or 'the tragedy'. Isn't that right, mother? There was 'before the tragedy' and 'after the tragedy'. The 'incident' or the 'tragedy' happened in winter with no warning signs. At least for me, it happened that way.

Hannah: You were too young to pick up on the nuances, and the decline, although slight, in his behavior.

Nicole: I later heard from my mother, that there had been hints. This came as a total surprise to me, out of the blue. For years I didn't understand what had happened, not until I was older; but I think what makes our story unique is that my sister and I witnessed what happened. In other words, something happened at home and we saw it happen. One would assume that there wasn't much left to understand since we saw him commit suicide – but I still don't understand. Sometimes you see something, you're supposed to understand, but I didn't understand.

Hannah: Who understood...?

Nicole: It is unfathomable. We lived on the fourth floor. It was a cold winter's night in February, when paraffin heaters were still in use in homes. We had a type of chimney... and... there was something going on between our father and mother...

Hannah: What happened was like a scene from a thriller. Today it isn't so hard for me to describe the incident. Two weeks prior to it happening I had been in hospital, nothing serious, but I had been away from home for two weeks. In retrospect those two weeks were critical for us. He was alone and took care of the girls on his own while I was in hospital. I subsequently learnt from my own mother that every night he would shut himself up in our bedroom. I knew nothing of this and only later the impact of those two weeks on the suicide became clear...after he did it. We were also unaware that he was having problems at work; he didn't share these with us. I knew that he was disgruntled but I didn't know that there had been problems between him and others workers. I have to say I was somewhat egocentric, as I thought mainly of myself. I had a really comfortable life. He made a good living, we had a nice group of friends, we enjoyed ourselves, we went out, celebrated, and life just rolled along so I didn't delve or ask too many questions.

It was a Wednesday and we went shopping in the market to buy things for the weekend, for the Sabbath when suddenly, while we were shopping, he kissed me... but there was something strange about it.

We returned home and began preparing dinner... our regular routine. He began cutting up the salad. I hope I remember it all accurately. Suddenly we heard a terrible scream. He stood there with the knife in his hand and then he ran after me with the knife. I tried to stay calm but I ran away from him and hid on the porch in shock. Then I ran into the bedroom and lay down on the bed. I don't know how other people feel in this situation, but I lay there as if my body wasn't my own. I didn't move – till he fell. Nicole can continue the rest of the story. The whole terrible tragedy... the jump, it happened before their very eyes. They saw it all.

Nicole: It's strange, it is difficult each time I go back to the incident. I remember the doors closing, and our mother running away. And then... the paraffin heater was standing under the window. He stopped chasing our mother, climbed onto the heater and from there to the window. Our apartment was four stories high. I remember my sister and me trying to pull him back. I was there, and the feeling of helplessness – I tried to pull him back but he dropped and fell. He screamed and that was it.

My sister had needed his help earlier that evening with bible study homework, and she remembers that he hadn't been speaking clearly. I remember how we were after that, we ran to our mother lying on the bed, trying to protect her.

Hannah: They took him to a hospital in Jaffa...but he arrived there completely crushed from the fall. There was no way to save him. Before it all started he tried to call his parents. Perhaps he wanted to say goodbye to them, I don't know. Or perhaps he was looking for a way out. But it was our bad luck that they weren't home.

Nicole: I remember a lot of crying. Nothing was clear to me. Everything and everyone around me was in a state of confusion.

Hannah: I didn't cry.

Nicole: It was sort of chaotic. I wasn't at the funeral, they didn't take me. But on the night it happened, policemen came to our house. That was difficult. Police – this means we've done something wrong, it's as if there's a blot on our family. For years this was a really heavy burden to bear and we didn't tell a soul; we kept it buried deep inside.

Hannah: Today I feel that I dealt with it the right way. To sweep the tragedy under the carpet wouldn't be right but because I was a teacher I believed that the good of the children came first.

Nicole: We really were very good girls. I only realize now how much this affects everything in our lives, the ramifications of his suicide affects everything.

Hannah: We returned to our daily routine fairly quickly.

Nicole: Yes, but it was only a pretense... the ground shook beneath us, but all in all it seemed to work fairly well. Grandmother (my mother's mother) came to help, and everything was fine. As if...

Hannah: We were lucky because my mother sacrificed a great deal. She came to live with us for almost five years. He was young, what kind of pension could a man of thirty three have had? We had to earn enough to keep the home going, we had to look good – and I couldn't fall apart.

Nicole: I always had the feeling that at home we weren't allowed to show signs of sadness and this really affected me. We had to pretend that everything was ok, that we were in control, that everything was just fine and we weren't allowed to fall apart.

Hannah: In actual fact, your difficulties were greater than mine. After all, I was only his wife; you were his flesh and blood.

Nicole: Not only 'after all' but it's true that I felt like an orphan without a father, I felt like damaged goods.

Hannah: It's important to discuss the gossip. Everyone looks for reasons and somehow these stories reached us too. It was because he argued with Hannah... ah; she probably cheated on him... all those kinds of stories. If I'd been fat and ugly they wouldn't have spoken like that, but I tried my best to put up a good front.

The situation was like this. I felt three things (puts up three fingers): shame, anger, and frustration. That's it. Maybe because of the anger I couldn't relate to the romantic aspect of our lives together and to the sadness of lost love. These feelings were blurred by my frustration and anger. The anger related to the act itself, leaving a wife and young children at this critical point in their lives.

Nicole: I, as the 'daughter of' wasn't angry with him. I identified with the tormented artist, and that's why I wasn't angry.

Hannah: I was so frustrated because he had such potential, and he squandered it. He could have made money, he had a good profession, but he didn't care about that.

Nicole: I remember that my father had a drawer, with all his things, a huge drawer. Inside was his portfolio, his pencils, his handwriting, poetry he loved, poems he wrote... the drawer was filled with him. When I wanted to recall my father's scent, I could open the drawer, inhale, and feel his presence.

Hannah: Actually last month I went looking through his drawer to find an answer to what he had done. Not in order to cling to the memories but rather to find clues to what might have led him to do it. I was left relatively unscathed by the incident. But the girls paid a high price. I buried myself in my work, I wanted to succeed. Lucky for them they were good girls.

Nicole: Maybe not 'lucky for them', as we demanded nothing, but it was like a volcano just smoldering beneath the surface... during my school years I found it difficult to cope emotionally. I was popular, and I was one of the best students, but the minute the word 'father' was mentioned, I felt terrible. I wanted the earth to swallow me up.

Hannah: The type of death isn't important. Children whose fathers fall in battle also suffer.

Nicole: We actually had an orphan in our class whose father died in the war. Can you believe this... I was jealous of him. I discussed this with my sister; how we wished our father had died in battle. What has been wearing me down all these years is the secret, and how the secret has affected me here (indicates her heart) – the secret and the shame. I was so ashamed.

I remember feeling that something was wrong with my family. I was so angry that in my home things were different; that we had a secret. Secrets – secrets – secrets, we weren't allowed to talk about it. I didn't ask my mother questions. She told us, when you miss him you can look at photographs.

Hannah: Something happened and I couldn't explain it to *myself,* so how could I explain it to you?

Nicole: Living with uncertainty was the most difficult thing for me. Because of that, to this day I'm afraid of the unknown. I'm afraid that some tragedy is just around the corner, waiting to happen, and I am unprepared. I would like to be totally prepared for every eventuality. Before giving birth I needed to know everything. I read all the books and I'm sure it's because I'm afraid of being caught off guard.

Hannah: The relationship between fathers and daughters is different to the relationship between mothers and daughters. A girl gets a lot of security from being hugged by her father, especially if he likes to hug and kiss and be affectionate. His absence has created in you…

Nicole: …a feeling of insecurity, of a bottomless pit. Everything was fine until seventh grade. Then suddenly things went wrong, I started to have feelings of guilt and shame…

Hannah: The relationship with his parents was quite problematic as he was an only child (Nicole laughs: "of a Polish mother"). He was their whole world. Even after we were married, his mother would tell me how to behave towards him. After his death she ignored us. She wanted no contact with us. She never came to our home. Her husband, on the other hand, felt he had become the man of the house, the father, in our home. He was a wonderful person. He took care of all our needs, worrying about the conservatory for the girls, academic institutions, a new piano and even a scholarship in his son's name.

Nicole: I missed my father at my final recital, at my graduation from university, he wasn't there. At my wedding, obviously… but events related to music – he should have been there with me… and he wasn't. I searched in 'dad's drawer' for a thread, for something aimed at me. I read everything I could in an attempt to understand who he was. But I was left with an enigma. Mother said he was a happy person, but then in my mind, why would a happy person commit suicide. Obviously people are both. I can also be happy and sad. There were times that I acted like a joker– this also became a type of defense, so no one would see my sadness… But eventually the time came when I had to deal with the question, 'Who am I, what am I?' When I wanted intimacy in my relationships, I realized that the time had come when I could no longer hide behind a mask. I didn't really feel good about myself. I guess it was insecurity.

After high school I went into the army (army service is compulsory in Israel). In the army I had lots of problems. It's not quite clear to me why it was so hard for me. Just being in that framework was very difficult for me. I saw others supported by family. There was something missing for me. The officers' course is really difficult and I had to give lectures but I didn't do this as well as I should have and I didn't complete the officers' course. Things didn't seem improve so I decided to check out what was happening to me.

When I was about twenty four or twenty five, I went to therapy. I found a therapist who really helped me. I was with her for a few years, and during this time, when I was about twenty seven, I met my husband. I really wanted to get married. I wanted to be 'okay' and I wanted children. I had always worked with children as a music teacher, and the connection between the children and music made me feel loved. It filled a need in me, to feel loved all the time, be hugged and experience happiness and joy...

Hannah: She takes after her father, the warmth, the happiness...

Nicole: I was the happiest person in the world when the children were born. Even today, my two children are an amazing source of joy to me. I think the fact that we didn't talk very much in my home was a red flag for me. In my home I am going to make sure that everything is out in the open, there will be no holy cows. No way. If my child asks a question there will always be an open channel of dialogue between us.

Hannah: Hold on a moment, I don't understand what you mean. Speak *to whom*?

Nicole: To the kids.

Hannah: You - with the children?

Nicole: Yes.

Hannah: But how can you compare? It was different for me, there was a block...

Nicole: I'm not comparing. I am saying that *because* of what happened to me, it is important that in my home, things will be different... because of the feeling I had of living with many unanswered questions.

Hannah: I think that the reason I didn't speak to you wasn't because of the suicide. It was because we were from another generation. But... I also felt I had nothing to say. When you speak to children you have to have something to say, something to strengthen them. I had nothing to say. The only thing I could say to you was, "We have to deal with this, let's show the world that we can manage." I had nothing more than that to say.

Nicole: Okay, but I'm talking about my needs, something huge was missing for me. There was a black hole, with a question mark.

Hannah: I can't know what it's like to be in your shoes and experience what you felt. But to look your child in the eye, and to see what your father did on that night – that's unfathomable, it's horrific the chance of that happening is one in a million. There are many cases of suicide but they don't happen right in front of the children.

Nicole: I assume that in all cases there are many questions.

Hannah: When it doesn't happen in front of the children, one can always 'bluff'. One can always lie...

Nicole: You know mum, once soon after it happened, I asked you what happened. And you answered, that he was ill.

Hannah: That is true, to a certain extent...

Nicole: Yes, but a child's mind works like this... sick? More questions... things weren't clear to me.

Hannah: Today I understand that I was incapable of explaining what he did. I had no answers. I met with a psychologist a week after 'the incident', but that particular psychologist didn't help me. He started to analyze my husband...and that didn't help me. Perhaps I had to hear from someone who understood the soul of a child, who could have helped me to deal with it. If circumstances had been different I would have coped better. If I had been a widow for other reasons I wouldn't have found it so difficult. Perhaps I would have found another way. It may have been possible to build a different life for myself had 'it' not happened at home.

Nicole: But that's how it happened...

Hannah: When I myself had no answers how could I provide answers to others? There are just the assumptions. One could assume a thousand different things but he took the secrets with him. It was impossible to say to a child, your father is the guilty one, not you. I definitely couldn't say that. The girls shouldn't have felt ashamed, but the feelings were overpowering.

When I said that he was sick I couldn't go into details. But in some ways suicide is a disease, a certain type of disease. To this day I believe, and we have spoken of it many times, that the final step wasn't premeditated because if someone intends to commit suicide it is hard for me to believe that he would do it the way he did... so cruelly, openly in front of his wife and in the presence of his daughters, it's too hard to believe. Also the confused things he said...I believe something happened to his brain.

Nicole: When I started to tell my friends about it, there was a time I wanted them to feel a little sorry for me. Up until then I had had to be strong and so these other feelings had been locked away. Now I wanted some pity. In my childhood I didn't feel I was pitied, it almost felt as if nothing had happened... but suddenly, after many years...

Hannah: Don't you remember that immediately after... some kids came to see you, they brought you gifts?

Nicole: (laughs) I love you mother...that was nice – but, gifts? They don't make up for other things.

Hannah: But what does an eight year old child want? She wants presents! At that time you didn't feel you needed attention. What you were getting was enough for you. I had a feeling that the sooner we returned to a regular routine, the better it would be. If we didn't move on with our lives we would never survive the crisis.

Nicole: That's exactly it; I had to be happy, I had to show that I was fine.

Hannah: But as my daughter you could have come to cry on my shoulder.

Nicole: Oh, I could have...

Hannah: I simply didn't know how to explain my belief that one doesn't have to explain to the children what happened to their father. The children saw *what* he did, but *why* he did it ... there were no answers for that. I admit now that I may not have dealt with things in the best way but I did the best I could, I did what I thought at the time was the best for the girls. The relationship between husbands and wives is different to that between fathers and daughters. I assumed that since I managed to cope so quickly, the girls could too... perhaps I shouldn't have made that assumption. I don't know what they felt about me. Perhaps they were critical.

Nicole: When I became a mother I felt very close to you.

Hannah: When he died, I was thirty four and a half. Today there are women at this age who are newly married but I had already been married for fifteen years. I was still a young woman. We were very close. We were both born here in Israel, we loved the same things, and we had a good life together.

I don't want to go over the despair and anger, but I had my needs. I needed to stand on my own two feet again. I said to myself okay, he's dead; it's like closing a door and opening another door. Now I have to start a new life, and will not stay stuck in my old life. I started going out. I met people, and my life began to take shape. I didn't marry again, that's true. Perhaps it's a shame because today at sixty seven, it's hard. At the age of forty, fifty, I had a good life. I cannot say that because of him my life was ruined. The girls made me happy, they went to university, got married, had children, and I had all the good things life has to offer. I enjoyed myself, had some romantic experiences, it wasn't bad...

There is no doubt that his memory is still alive, but for me the incident was much less traumatic than it was for the girls. If I did something wrong, I can only ask for their forgiveness. I thought that if I helped meet all their physical needs, clothes, and shoes to wear, everything to make life comfortable, a roof over their heads, movies, theatre, if there was no change from what had been before – then everything would be fine.

Nicole: Our well organized home did provide a feeling of security.

Hannah: I loved going out, but I also loved our home. From my point of view, life returned to normal and I didn't think that for them the trauma would continue for much longer, or that it might never let up. From my point of view I recovered but I also know why. There is an enormous difference between us.

Nicole: People always tell me that I am a good listener. I am always the friend who tries to save the world. After many years I understood that I couldn't save the ones I should have saved. I save myself by helping others. The need to listen, to understand what happens to others, is stronger than I am. And I am sure it's all related. My mother tells me that before it happened I was a quiet shy girl. As a result of his suicide these traits became stronger, but therapy helped me give up the feeling of being a victim. The psychologist said something which made an impression on me to this very day: "You were sacrificed when you were eight; what happened, happened. You were a victim, but there is no need to drag this feeling of victimization with you throughout your life." This sentence was a turning point for me and headed me in a new direction.

Until I was twenty four, everything was hidden. Everything started from 'the event'. But I told myself to take responsibility and not blame my past for everything. I had to get over it. Till the age of twenty four I was like a little girl. I didn't complete the officer's course, because of my life story. Today I have managed to separate the two, what happened with him is *connected to me*, but it is *not me*. I need to be open and not secretive, to be authentic. That's why it was so important for me to meet you, someone who had experienced something similar. I feel we are (searches for the words) ... kind of kindred spirits and I couldn't see that life could be beautiful. Today the relationships in our nuclear family are close and supportive. Today, mother, I can come to you and cry...

Hannah: When I went out with men, I never told them the truth. I also saw the suicide as something negative. Not that I thought I was to blame, but I tried to imagine how people would react. I went out with a guy; when I told him that my husband had committed suicide, I could just picture what was going through his mind... if her husband did this, who knows what she did to him... (laughs).

Nicole: On the other hand, I as 'the daughter of' told my husband. He knows.

Hannah: How could he not know? Describe what happened in the workshop when you met him.

Nicole: I took part in a weekend workshop; there was an exercise in psychodrama where we had to tell our story. I had to choose someone to play the part of my father, and I chose him (my future husband). I didn't know him then. He wasn't alarmed; he was able to deal with it. At some unconscious level I wanted to find someone older so I guess this had something to do with my choice.

I've always had a need to be strong as well as the need to excel. This way I feel that I don't need anyone else. I prefer to be needed by others and not be dependent. I grew up thinking that without a man my mother is only half a person. I'm driven to succeed so that I won't be dependent. For many years I didn't feel sorry for myself. I refused to allow self-pity to be part of me. Along with all the negative things connected with this tragedy, it has also had some positive influences on my life. The search for meaning, the type of listening that gives me amazing feedback, also excelling in what I do. The drive to grow. In my mind these traits are a kind of gift. What does it mean that my father didn't find meaning in life? For me, there is no such thing as 'life without meaning'. I believe that one doesn't look for meaning in life, one *creates* meaning. I want to nurture relationships; this is important to me, and it is especially important not to keep secrets. When you bring things out into the open you discover that the demons aren't so bad after all. You look at the pictures, laugh, feel happy, and then you understand that life is good...

Hannah: Sometimes I think of him, and wonder what was so bad for him, he really lacked nothing. Was he short of money? No he wasn't. Did he have debts? No. He had a home and no mortgage, a house full of friends, why did this happen when everything was so good? It's hard for me to understand what went wrong.

Nicole: What a loss, he was a really good man, he was so noble and proud, and everyone respected him... and suddenly everything explodes in your face.

GRIEVING PROCESS

I n a person's lifetime, one of the most difficult experiences is losing a close relative, and the process of coping with this loss is called the 'grieving process'. This term defines particular stages of grief but these phases do not necessarily follow step by step in a specific order. The grieving process is generally made up of four phases: shock and denial, anger, guilt and depression, acceptance and integration of the loss. Most people experience all these stages in one way or another.

This can be seen in Rachel's outburst when while talking about her daughter's suicide, she exclaimed... "Couldn't she wait?" Similarly Hannah's feelings of anger at her husband prevented her from mourning the feelings connected to the loss of the romantic side of their relationship which had been such an important part of her marriage.

According to Elizabeth Kubler-Ross [31] the grieving process enables mourners to cope with the fears that close contact with death evokes, and it facilitates expression of one's feelings concerning these fears. The purpose of mourning ceremonies is to allow the relatives to express their feelings and fears, and not prevent or suppress pain. Only when one is able to cope with the pain will the mourner be able to separate from the deceased. Usually the process ends when mourners are able to establish a routine and feel that life has returned to normal, both physically and emotionally. The time frame for this process varies from person to person. The end of the process does not necessarily mean that the mourner returns to the same way of life they had before the death, but they do return to a routine, even if it is different than before. When the grieving process runs its course it is characterized by a weakened, dulled sense of the grief and sorrow, together with an increased feeling of vitality and pleasure in life.

---

31   Kubler-Ross, E. (1969). On Death and Dying. London: Collier McMillan

In a recently published study, Stroebe[32] re-examined the question, asked earlier by Engel in his break-through work from 1961, "Is grief a disease?" In addition, he asked whether long-term outcomes of grief may be considered a mental disorder? There are many ceremonies that are part of the grieving process and they have a time frame. They begin immediately after the death of a relative. These ceremonies include the funeral, different forms of mourning and expressions of sympathy, condolences, memorial events, and annual memorial services. All these situations encourage and motivate relatives and friends to talk about the deceased, share their loss and express their feelings. These ceremonies usually follow a standard pattern and include specific customs, depending on religion, tradition, and community practices. These prescribed practices make it easier for the mourners, as they provide guidelines for their behavior. Processing grief is essential for what they must go through, and it enables the mourners to separate, thereby facilitating closure of the physical and emotional cycle they shared.

In addition to the suffering and pain of losing a loved one, the grief experienced by relatives of people who have committed suicide is compounded, intensified, and complicated by the other emotions such as shame, guilt, and anger. They may wonder if there was something in their behavior which might have triggered the suicide. At the same time there is always the question in the back of their minds as to whether there are other family members who are at risk of committing suicide. Interviewees I met spoke at length about feelings of anger and guilt, and the difficulty of talking about the suicide itself. These difficulties are often eased when survivors join support groups. There, they say, among others like themselves, they feel free from the stigma.

The reaction to, and effect of, suicide is experienced differently in the different groups of survivors. Parents who have lost a child to suicide suffer a double trauma. They suffer both from losing their child, and the fact that it was a suicide. In many cases they feel that they failed in their primary duty, namely protecting and keeping their child safe. The parents are constantly filled with questions and feelings of guilt, and examine their behavior over and over again, agonizing over every word and act, even the most insignificant ones, to find something that might have caused the suicide.

Alison Wertheimer,[33] a researcher whose sister committed suicide,

32   Stroebe, M. (2015). Is grief a disease? Why Engel posed the question. *Omega* 71(3)
33   Wertheimer, A. (1991). A Special Scar – the Experience of people Bereaved by Suicide. New York: Routledge

interviewed siblings of people who committed suicide. In memory of her sister, Wertheimer wrote the book *A Special Scar* in which she included findings from the interviews. One important finding was that because of the silence surrounding suicide in general, there was no one to guide those who were grieving, no one to tell them what a 'common reaction' is. The title of the book refers to the special scar that suicide leaves on survivors for many years, a scar which is at the same time hidden yet indelible.

In many cases suicide survivors do not, even partially, go through the standard grieving process. As they often harbor the secret, and suffer from the social stigma attached to suicide, they do not go through a healthy process of mourning and ultimately suffer long term emotional repercussions as they are unable and have no avenue to express their grief. They often find it difficult to share their feelings with others, including family members. The grieving process resulting from suicide is different because the death is deliberate and self-inflicted. Even in cases where the suicide was at least partly expected, after prior suicide attempts, or severe mental illness, it is a shock. As one of the interviewees said about her mother's suicide, although it was always a possibility, when it happened, it was a shock for the family. Even when a suicide occurs after many years of mental illness, and even if the deceased had threatened to do it, it is very difficult to believe that someone would deliberately take their own life. It is a phenomenon which contradicts human nature and the primal instinct for survival.

In any case of bereavement, other than death from suicide, there are mourning ceremonies, with clear behavioral codes. There are also standard traditional condolence expressions such as "May you know no more sorrow." In the case of a suicide there are no ceremonies or rituals guiding one's behavior. What should one say? Will it be right or wrong to mention the deceased, the circumstances of their death, or the very word 'suicide'? All these make the grieving process for suicide different and more difficult. The purpose of the ceremonies and the annual memorials is to create a place where it is appropriate to talk about the dead, evoke common memories and thus aid the family in its time of grief. The lack of grieving ceremonies in the case of suicide increases the pressures on the family.

Colin Pritchard claims that there are people who do not want to attract attention after a suicide in their family. This enables and legitimizes the reaction of the community to ignore these families and their pain. It also inhibits people from offering assistance which could somewhat alleviate the suffering of the family. He talks about the long lasting impact on the families, sometimes for many years, and defines the families as living in a double-risk situation due to grief and ignorance. Pritchard explains that in many cases the suicide is not the end, but rather the beginning of more suffering.

Many of my interviewees expressed similar feelings. It is not that the family prefers to suffer quietly; not having grieving ceremonies, and the exclusion of the dead person, are all part of the unresolved processing of the death. Marsha, for example, said she did not go to her father's grave for 20 years saying "He doesn't deserve it." After 20 years her grieving process was still stuck in the anger phase.

Two sources of assistance have emerged to help survivors deal with the shame and stigma surrounding suicide, and they reinforce and enhance the experience of the different (or in some cases total lack of) grieving process. In many countries support groups have formed where suicide survivors can meet other people who have been through the same experience and where they don't have to battle with the shame, and the social price of exposing their story. In addition opportunities provided through use of the web, ranging from use of relevant sites and participation in virtual communities to involvement in social networks and active participation in groups have enabled survivors to share and express their pain, while at the same time remaining anonymous if they so desire.

One of these sites[34] provides a 'do and don't' list for both mourners and people who wish to provide support. In the do list are things like accepting the volume of pain, being aware of support groups, respecting the need for grief, and 'listening with the heart'. The 'don't' list includes things like avoiding simplistic explanations, not using clichés, not saying that the deceased was insane or abnormal, and *never trying to take the pain from the grieving person.*

---

34 www.survivorsofsuicide.com. Retrieved 28.2.2016

FEELINGS TOWARDS THE DECEASED

I n his book *On the Nature of Suicide*[35] Edwin Shneidman claims that suicide survivors tend to hold strong feelings, especially of guilt and anger, towards the deceased, often for many years after the suicide. Albert Cain also refers to these feelings pointing out that the mourning process is similar for every death including death by suicide, but in the case of suicide, feelings of anger and guilt prevail and may last for many years following the death.

Anger

Anger directed at someone who has committed suicide is multi-faceted. There is anger at the act itself, and anger due to frustration and helplessness of being faced with an act one can neither understand nor explain. Furthermore the deceased leaves the relatives angry at the irreversibility of the act and angry for not allowing the relatives to save them. For this reason some of the interviewees called this 'an active death', not only because it was intentional, but also because the deceased continues to play a part in the lives of the bereaved. There is an ongoing dialog and argument with the deceased about what they did and this may continue for many years.

Associated with anger after the suicide is resentment which arises from the frustration of asking a question to which there is no answer: 'Why did you do it?' Anger is also linked with societal stigma and shame associated with suicide, and expressed in the question: Why did you do it *to me*? An unsolicited identity has been imposed on the survivors for the rest of their lives. Anger is directed against the deceased for compelling the family to become a part of his deed thus imposing the stigma upon them too.

Anger also arises from frustration felt by survivors who are unable

---

35   Edwin Shneidman, *On the nature of suicide,* San Francisco, Jossey Bass 1969

to understand why the deceased could find no other alternative to cope. A correlation was found between the ability to understand the deceased and the motive, and the presence or absence of anger. If one can understand the reasons leading to the suicide this may contribute to an understanding of the pain and sorrow which made the suicide unavoidable. However, the less comprehensible the pain and anguish of the deceased is to the survivors, the more anger they experience. This was clear from the interview with Leonora, when she stated that she could understand that for her mentally-ill mother, the option of living was the worst option, not the best one.

Guilt Feelings

Wrobleski and McIntosh conducted research among survivors who were members of the 'Minneapolis support group'[36]. They studied 159 males and females aged 16-77. 86% reported feelings of guilt following the suicide of their relative, regardless of the relationship, although the majority of the interviewees were parents, children, siblings and spouses. They found that survivors suffered from two types of guilt feelings: 67% blamed themselves for doing something which might have caused the suicide, and 11% blamed themselves for not doing enough to prevent it. 22% reported that they felt that others blamed them for the suicide.

There is a link between the position in the relationship of the survivor and the deceased, and the reflective guilt feelings about the suicide. *Parents* tend to feel extremely guilty for not having fulfilled their primary parental role in protecting their child's life. In many cases *spouses* feel that they were unsuccessful in building a strong loving relationship which could have eased their spouse's pain. Surprisingly, many *children* who have lost a parent to suicide suffer from guilt feelings even if they were very young at the time. For instance, when a husband commits suicide while his wife is pregnant the child born after the father's death may feel that the pregnancy with him or her was the trigger to the suicide. If children feel that the surviving parent has guilt feelings they may feel that they are a partner in that guilt.

After the death of a parent children may take on the responsibilities of the dead parent thereby growing up very quickly. In cases of suicide they may see themselves as being responsible, in hindsight, for things which occurred before taking on these responsibilities and thereby also for the suicide. They may even remember things that happened at home and in

---

36   A. Wrobleski and J.L. McIntosh, problems of suicide survivors: a survey report. *Israel Journal of Psychiatry and Related Sciences*, (24), 137-142, 1987.

drawing conclusions from this may believe that had they acted differently the suicide may have been prevented. After the suicide, relatives often torment themselves with ideas that there were hints and clues which they should have picked up and acted upon. Some of these clues are often explanations made only in retrospect and not real clues which could have prevented the suicide. Nevertheless the survivors are left with guilt feelings for not identifying the risk or for not persevering in their efforts to prevent the suicide. Another aspect of guilt is conjecture that by committing suicide, the deceased was punishing the loved ones for something they (the survivors) did.

Susan

I met Susan after publishing a request in the newspaper, for suicide survivors who would be willing to take part in, and be interviewed for, a research project.

Initially, hers was the only response I received.

I was born in South America. I left home at twenty, at the time when people around us started to disappear. My brother and I were forced to leave South America and we were put on a plane and sent to a kibbutz in Israel. After a short time my brother returned to South America but I loved Israel and stayed. I felt at home and was grateful to be accepted. When I eventually went back to visit my parents I found them both in a state of depression. I felt guilty for having left them alone and therefore felt I was not a good daughter. I went to therapy to help me cope with my guilt feelings.

Soon after I married, my husband and I went to visit my parents. Shortly after that my father committed suicide. Actually I am not sure that he really committed suicide, even though throughout his life he often threatened to kill himself to get me to do what he wanted. At home he would act strangely but to the outside world he seemed normal; he was like Dr. Jekyll and Mr. Hyde. Later someone explained to me that this was an illness and that it is not unusual for someone to act out his anger at home. This behavior intensified when my brother and I left home. I felt guilty that we went away and weren't there for him at the end. Before his death he had been acting irrationally and was prone to violence, so a doctor came to the house and prescribed tranquilizers. He had always relied fairly heavily on alcohol. He was taken to hospital after taking tranquilizers together with alcohol, but it was too late. It was a tragic end. On the basis of the post-mortem the hospital cited cause of death as suicide.

Before my eldest daughter was born, my mother committed suicide. There is no doubt that she *really* committed suicide. I believe my father drove her crazy. She died eight years after he did. Even though I often think about my parents, I can't recall the exact dates of their deaths. I feel no pity when I think about my mother's death, only anger. My mother jumped from the seventh floor of a building so there was no doubt that she wanted to kill herself. She was full of life and yet she was very immature. She had been hospitalized several times. I was far away. Basically, that's the story.

I was raised in the shadow of suicide threats. My mother killed herself unexpectedly, but for years my father threatened to kill himself. In actual fact I pulled him back from the window a few times, but I think he wanted to be saved. His brother also committed suicide by choking himself with a belt that his daughter gave him for his birthday. He made his intentions very clear. My cousin, his daughter, was near him at the time. These were terrible experiences and everything about our family was shrouded in mystery. My brother and I were aware of our father's threats. We understood that if we didn't do things the way he wanted, he might end his life.

I think suicide is the most aggressive thing one can do to one's family. It has far reaching ramifications. Ever since my mother jumped I have been afraid of heights. When my children climb things and look down I experience real anxiety attacks. This is just one way in which I have been affected.

I often think... My mother, my father, and my uncle did it, why in heaven's name won't I? Why not my children? I am scared. What would I do if my daughter committed suicide? What if I had been different, what if my mother had been different, perhaps all this would not have happened? Everything makes me feel guilty and afraid. Everything! My children, the house, my friends, work... guilt feelings are central to my life and to my cousin's life too. I live filled with guilt, fear, tension, sadness, and anger all the time. Anger together with sadness and fear, engulfs me, fear that someone will die. I am afraid of death, the death of my brother, myself, thoughts of how my parents died, what happened to them and I panic when I hear stories of disasters. I'm not ashamed but I won't talk about it with my children. It's not an easy topic to discuss because of society's attitude. It's an end like any other end, but there is no one to talk to about it.

In the Jewish religion if someone commits suicide they are buried outside the boundaries of the cemetery. In order to have my father buried in the cemetery we had to donate his organs. Until this happened to our family I didn't know that people who committed suicide were not buried within the walls of the cemetery. They agreed to bury him inside, but we had to pay. When my mother died she was buried alongside my father with no questions asked. In South America the topic of suicide is discussed much more openly.

In Israel I felt tainted. I once applied to live in a small village community. When I related the story of my mother (I only told them about my mother) in the interview with the acceptance committee, a very nice lady told me not to tell anyone else as they may not accept me. I thought that perhaps they might think that suicide runs in families or that people in my family are insane. When a suicide occurs there is more involved than just the secret. It's something you carry with you throughout your whole life.

I didn't name any of my children after him. I don't know why we should feel so ashamed. It's not as if we did anything bad; we didn't do anything unprecedented.

Every suicide story is unique. A friend of ours just committed suicide while his wife was pregnant. He was a man who appeared to have everything. It was unforgivable. His wife was pregnant – how could he do it? How could he do it to her? He hurt her, he attacked the whole family. I see suicide as an attack which destroys an entire family.

Perhaps it's a form of mental illness and yet the people in the family need to act as if everything is ok. It takes a lot of courage to talk openly about the fact that someone in your family committed suicide. You're really putting other people's reactions to the test. We all have to pretend that we are perfect. I think our upbringing makes it difficult for people to talk about their feelings.

When I read your ad in the newspaper, I procrastinated... but then I decided to call you. I was really scared. I didn't even tell my husband. He comes from a very stable family. It was only after you and I had arranged a meeting that I told him. He was worried and couldn't understand why I needed to do this. I explained that I couldn't talk to him about it and in fact there was no one I felt comfortable or able to talk to. I thought it was very brave of you to advertise the way you did. I wish people could talk freely about everything.

I am angry and full of hatred. One shouldn't say that about one's father but I hate him. I blame him. Even if I wanted to have memorial days for my parents I just couldn't do it. I feel that my identity is tainted. I always envied my girlfriends who had a father and a mother. I wanted so much to have a normal home. I looked at the way other fathers behaved with their children. I am constantly preoccupied with questions such as how to avoid making the mistakes my parents made? I try to be open and encourage my children to talk to me about anything. I don't want to harm them the way I was harmed and I don't want the mental instability from my past to affect them. My daughter has started to smoke, she is 16. I remember when I started smoking, thinking that if my father found out, he'd kill himself... I hope my kids won't be afraid to talk to me. I want them to feel that they can be open with me because I won't commit suicide.

When my mother came to visit me in Israel she was already unwell. She had suffered from depression in the past but in general she coped and lived a normal life. We prepared a room for her in our house. While she was with us she tried to kill herself. She took an overdose of pills. I had to take her to the hospital. If she really wanted to do it, why didn't she finish the job? There were children in the house, babies all around, how inconsiderate! It's true, she was slightly eccentric, but she functioned, she cooked, and then suddenly at six in the evening she decided to commit suicide! We sent her to a psychiatrist. I really believe that behind each suicide there is a form of mental illness even with people who seem to do it spontaneously. It is an act which contradicts the survival instinct and opposes human nature, where the will to live and the desire to survive are of primary importance.

I also wanted to meet you to confirm that I am not alone and that there are more people who feel and worry as I do. I wanted to know that this has happened to others and not only to me and my family. I think it is very important to raise public awareness, to talk, and to alleviate the fears of the survivors. There will always be people who commit suicide, but perhaps this will help the survivors.

When my husband talked about my parents' suicide with our daughter, I was very angry. It is *my* story, and I felt it was up to me to decide when, how much to tell, and how to talk to her about it. He didn't understand why I was willing and even wanted, to be interviewed. I explained that your father committed suicide too and this made it comfortable for me to talk to you. I didn't feel that you were judging me.

I know that I'll have to talk about it with my kids one day, but at the moment they are too young. I did talk to my eldest daughter about my parents' suicide after my husband brought it up, but we haven't spoken of it any more. It is as if they never existed. I didn't cry when they died and this makes me feel guilty too.

PREOCCUPATION WITH REASONS FOR THE SUICIDE

A lbert Cain said that suicide survivors are preoccupied with questions as to why the suicide occurred, especially when there is no suicide note or comprehensible explanation. He calls it 'the agonizing question', the question that is repeatedly asked but will, in fact, never be answered. Even if the person who committed suicide left a note, the survivors often find it hard to understand and accept the reasons for actually doing it. For people who have never experienced severe depression, it is extremely difficult to understand the magnitude of feelings of helplessness or hopelessness which make a person decide that taking their own life is the best alternative to the current situation.

When no answer to the question 'Why did he/she do it?' can be found, the question remains open ended and relatives search for various ways to answer it. When the reason is known, and especially when it is not the first case of suicide in the family, the survivors question whether there are genetic factors which affect some of the family members or whether this might be a family phenomenon. There are families in which recurring cases of suicide occur. From time to time a story emerges of a hidden or forgotten relative who 'probably' committed suicide. In these cases where there is secrecy and forgetfulness, there is an aura of mystery which further adds to the taboo surrounding the phenomenon of suicide. There are many factors which may lead to suicide: depression, various life crises, mental illness, or other reasons leading to feelings of helplessness. In some cases suicide notes help to lessen the mystery, but do not solve it completely. Adam described the letter his father left, as 'a letter which explained nothing'. When Lisa's parents showed me her letter they claimed that it did not explain why such a gifted young woman would choose this solution. Her explanation that she couldn't take it anymore meant nothing for them.

In many cases a person plans the suicide in advance, leaving time to try and explain it to the relatives. Meryl told me that her father carried his suicide letter around in his pocket for nine months, until he was 'ripe' to actually commit suicide. The suicide letter will never fully explain the act because, as many interviewees put it, it is incomprehensible. A suicide letter which says that the person could no longer bear their suffering only magnifies the survivors' guilt feelings. In other cases the deceased asks for the family's forgiveness in the letter, or hints towards the future. In the final analysis the question 'why did he do it?' remains very difficult to answer.

Survivors often express the wish for just one more opportunity to talk to the deceased about the suicide. This meeting would also allow for an appropriate farewell which was denied. This fantasy embodies the wish to have the person back and thereby repair the family story which was irreparably damaged with the suicide.

The genetic question of suicide is an important one. Some survivors feel that suicide is a family trait. This causes anxiety on two levels: anxiety that suicide runs in the family, and anxiety that they or others in the family might also commit suicide.

When talking about her father, Meryl raised the fact that his mother was really unbalanced. She expressed her fear that there was a possible genetic factor because there were also problems with other relatives in her family. "I hope that we're all healthy", she said.

Maya had been raised by her mother in a single parent family. After her mother's suicide she went to visit her mother's family who lived abroad. She discovered that there was mental-illness in the family. She had always known where her father lived so when she was a university student she went to visit him. She wanted to trace the genetic makeup on her father's side to see if she had anything to fear. She wanted to know if there were mental problems on his side too. When she met her father she found a person with no history of suicide in the family. As she has put it, "my genes on his side are fine."

Trying to discover the motive and trigger for the suicide is a search for a reason which might give meaning to an incomprehensible act. It is a never ending search and there appears to be no logical explanation. The absence of an adequate explanation means that the family is never able to emotionally bury the dead. This in turn leads to an unfulfilled and never ending mourning processs.

BEREAVED SONS AND DAUGHTERS

What happens to children when they find that a parent has suddenly vanished from their lives? The British researcher, Colin Pritchard, refers to collective childhood memory where we learn for the first time the significance of death and through this experience, the anxiety of knowing that our parents are likely to die too. Loss of a parent, regardless of one's age, arouses the most primal fears and anxieties. These fears and anxieties are increased when the abandonment of the child by the parent is deliberate. Children are left lacking the support of the very person who would naturally have helped them traverse the space between themselves and their loss.

Some researchers claim that children who have lost a parent to suicide experience post traumatic responses which include denial of the event, suppression of feelings and thoughts regarding the event, and concern about further imminent tragedies.[37] Adults who have lost a family member to suicide seek comfort in attempting to understand the reason, from the perspective of the deceased, which led them to take their own life. For children, suicide in general, however particularly that of a parent, is experienced as a violent, emotionally laden act. It is experienced as a terrible act of abandonment and rejection and the child really has no means of dealing with this. The total belief children have of their own importance in the eyes of their parents is an existentially essential component of their overall emotional development.

In the case of parental suicide it is as if children learn that they were not important enough for the parent to choose life over death. Tamar Granot contends that this affects the very foundation of the child's existence. She

---

37 Pynoos, R.S. and Spencer, E. (1986). Special Intervention Programs for Child Witnesses to Violence. In M. Lystad (ed.). Violence in the Home: Interdisciplinary perspective. New York: Bruhner. 193-215

adds that in many cases the cause of death is often hidden from the child, becoming a burden, a secret waiting to be exposed, and to explode.[38]

Losing a parent is always a difficult and traumatic event for the child, who is left unprotected from the outside world. This is especially true in the case of suicide, when the child is left vulnerable, exposed, and filled with intense, incomprehensible feelings because of the suicide. A state of secrecy which prevents legitimate expression of these feelings is established. In some cases the child may not even be aware that such feelings exist.

A child whose need to mourn is denied valid expression, is also unable to express anger toward the parent who has died. In addition to anger (when the child 'dares' to be angry with the parent), guilt feelings may arise and these feelings too, are often denied legitimate expression. Susan was one of my first interviewees. Both her parents committed suicide. She describes the suicide of a parent as an "angry death, not a sad one."

Children respond to suicide in a variety of ways. First the child feels alone, abandoned by the parent. Then particularly during adolescence, in addition to feeling unloved and unwanted, the child is left with feeling as if he or she has no role model. Understanding the act of suicide allows the child to relate to the suicide from the parents' point of view. This somewhat reduces feelings of anger towards the parent and toward the act itself. Maya, another interviewee whose mother committed suicide after many years of mental illness, expressed an understanding for why her mother took her life.

There may be a relationship between the child's anger and an intuitive sense that the parent may commit suicide. This may be a result of many years of poor mental health or depression on the part of the parent, or following previous suicide attempts. In these instances the option of suicide is present within the family background, whether the parent has actively threatened to commit suicide or not. When the parent finally commits suicide, the fact that the child has been somewhat prepared for it means the anger associated with feelings of abandonment is diminished.

Children who have lost a parent to suicide are vulnerable to emotional difficulties in adolescence since in many cases the remaining parent and other family members are unable to

deal with these difficulties. Children's feelings towards the deceased are blocked, and at times they feel that they too might commit suicide when they reach the same age the parent was when he or she committed suicide. In

---

38 Tamar Granot, (2000) *Without You: The impact of loss and mourning on children and youth* .Jerusalem: Publication of the Ministry of Defense

the words of one of the interviewees Maya, "I thought that *this would happen* to me when I reached the age of thirty-three, which was the age my mother was when she committed suicide." Against the backdrop of the 'family myth', emotional difficulties are amplified. Nonverbal cues send a clear message that discussion of the deceased parent is not encouraged within or outside of the family.

Albert Cain[39], in his study of forty five children whose parents had committed suicide found that these children sensed that talking about the suicide at school was taboo. They therefore had no place where they were able to talk about it. Other research has found that in many cases children were unaware of the circumstances of the death and that some of them eventually only learnt of the suicide from people outside the family circle.

The book *Tale of Love and Darkness*[40] by Amos Oz is an excellent portrayal of the 'dead end street of sadness', of a child whose mother committed suicide. Oz writes: "I have hardly ever spoken about my mother till now, till I came to write these pages. Not with my father, or my wife, or my children or with anyone else." In a newspaper interview, the author's daughter Prof. Fania Oz-Zaltzberger, named after her grandmother who committed suicide, recounts that she only learned of the suicide when she was sixteen and came across a biographical sketch on her father in an English book.[41] When I gave this book to my sister as a gift I inscribed these words to her: "This is a book about families – and about us."

There are families in which the secret is kept for many years, sometimes for decades, where the parent is removed from the family narrative. In these cases children quickly discover the difference between the relative who is never referred to, as opposed to other relatives whose memories are honored and whose pictures are displayed in the home. Children know there is something irregular surrounding these 'unmentionable and unmentioned relatives'. This arouses curiosity with regard to those whose story has vanished from the family history. When children try to talk about the deceased they are often met with a wall of silence indicating that they are treading on dangerous ground. They soon realize that it is not worth exploring any further and in the face of this reaction children tend to stop questioning.

Often parents and relatives who refrain from speaking of the deceased

39   Cain, A. (2002). Children of Suicide: the Knowing and the Telling. Omega 65(2)124-136
40   Amos Oz, *A Tale of love and Darkness*, Jerusalem, Keter publishers 2002
41   Tigenboren, E. (16.3.2001). I am a genetic Autonomy. Yedioth Aharonoth – Shiva Yamim Daily publication, Israel.

do so with the best of intentions, in order to protect the child from the problematic, sensitive stories of the family. What this does not take into account is that others do speak of the suicide, and the child then hears of it outside the family. When this happens the child is left unprotected and ignorant of the true facts as these were not provided in the home. Previous consideration of this may well have protected the child from trauma caused by the revelation of the story in this manner.

As incredible as it may seem, sometimes the untold tale spans several generations. The relative who committed suicide may only return to the family narrative after many decades, if at all. Only then is one permitted to speak openly of the deceased. The child pays a heavy price for this secrecy as the positive aspects of the parent are not referred to and disappear into the family secret together with any other information about the parent.

The child learns that something so terrible and shameful happened that not only is it hidden from the outside world, but it is not even referred to at home and is hidden from family members wherever possible. For the child a significant feature of the shame of suicide is that it pervades the entire family. Since the child is unable to talk of the parent, the process of mourning is blocked, the child has no one to speak to, and therefore the child's ability to cope with the separation from the parent is not facilitated. When children are denied the proper channels for mourning, they are unable to separate from the parent and are also unable to separate from the continuing shame of an act for which they are not to blame. The secret is all encompassing and children feel that they are part of it. They often feel ashamed and therefore they too pay the social price.

Adam, whose father committed suicide when he was twelve and a half years old, remembers thinking then, that perhaps others saw his family as being 'crazy'. Thus the link between suicide, madness, and therefore mental illness, is established. Although his father committed suicide as a result of financial pressure, the act of suicide turned him into someone suffering from mental illness, and this, in turn, labeled the family. This is an excellent example of how a family becomes stigmatized. Some people do commit suicide as a result of mental illness and the stigma attached to mental illness then pervades the rest of the family too.

One way in which survivors deal with a stigma such as this is to obliterate the deceased by refusing to talk about him or her. Avoidance of questions dealing with the suicide creates a web of lies. For example, when asked about his father's suicide, Adam had two options: "I would say he was killed in a car crash, or I would change the subject." The first option Adam chose was to lie, to pretend there had been a 'legitimate' death. The second option available to him was to avoid the subject altogether.

Whether by telling a lie or changing the subject, a child must ultimately expend a lot of energy. This is all in an attempt to avoid dealing with the response of society should the true circumstances of the death of a parent be revealed. Adam speaks of his experiences. He remembers from an early age how the family was abandoned by friends following the suicide. Family members experience feelings of loneliness as a result of being abandoned even by closest friends. The family feels affiliated with a group who are avoided and rejected by others.

The stigma, the taboo, and the resulting transformation of the suicide into a secret, permeate the family experience as a whole. There is a preoccupation with the question: "What if they find out?" and intrigues of lies and secrets are thus created and perpetuated. The difficulties of dealing with the suicide are exacerbated by the attempt to conceal the suicide. It appears that children who do not speak of the suicide of a parent are unaware of the energy invested by the whole family in this attempt to conceal the truth. They know somehow, usually through nonverbal cues, that they are not permitted to reveal the facts outside of the family.

When the suicide is not addressed within the family, the child and the other survivors are unable to comfort each other. However it is clear that even when not referred to or spoken about, the deceased continues to exist within, and have an effect on, family life.

An excellent example of this can be seen in the interview with Hannah (the wife) and Nicole (the daughter).While Nicole complained that the home was filled with secrets, Hannah justified this saying that she was unable to explain to her daughters "that which she herself could not understand". She felt that perhaps her daughters needed an explanation of the facts, but she could not provide this explanation. They were, however, in need of *emotional* support so that they could be angry, could mourn, and could also understand why their father had vanished from their lives.

Marsha's father committed suicide when she was twelve. Marsha instinctively understood from her mother that she would be ostracized by the rest of the family if she exposed the true story. Revealing the suicide would be seen as a betrayal of the family ties so any discussion or reference to the memory of her father was avoided. Marsha's mother threatened to disown her if she revealed the facts of her father's suicide. Her mother's threat was effective, and to this day Marsha finds it difficult to divulge the secret of her father's death. Marsha has not yet told her children the truth about her father's death. She says "Until I tell them they will be spared from knowing that parents die... when they are able to understand, then I'll tell them..."

Both Susan's parents committed suicide. She emigrated from South America. She comments on how the attitudes of Israelis differ to those in her country of origin. She feels that in Israel suicide is considered a blot on the family name. From her experience and situations she saw around her, she believes that had she revealed the truth about her parents' suicides she may not have been accepted to live as a member of the communal settlement where she now lives.

Adam believed it was important to conceal the suicide from friends, and particularly from his girlfriend, in case they abandoned him.

Ron relates the way in which he learnt of his father's suicide. His story is repeated by other interviewees. "I only learnt of it from my girlfriend many years later. Just like that in a conversation she said, 'they say he committed suicide'." Ron felt that suddenly things began to make sense. In these few words he summed up one of the most difficult experiences of his life, trying to make sense of the insinuations and allusions to the hitherto untold story.

When the suicide of a parent is kept secret the child has no manner in which process the facts, even prior to the process of mourning itself. The child seeks ways of synthesizing the facts and confirming the suspected story. When no facts are readily available the child searches for every little detail in an attempt to coherently collate the missing pieces through hints and inferences until the story starts to make sense.

This was Ron's experience when he first learnt of his father's suicide from his girlfriend. Ultimately it did not come as a complete surprise to him. An innuendo which had previously alerted his attention suddenly made sense so he knew immediately that what he had just heard was true. However the stigma is so extensive that even though no longer a secret, to this day he still cannot speak freely of his father's suicide. Consequently, even after the secret is exposed, often purely by chance, the child is still alone in having to deal with the ramifications.

Keeping the facts hidden for so many years is a major cause of the difficulties experienced, even into adulthood, by the surviving relatives. Ron, whose father committed suicide when he was fourteen, thirty years prior to the interview, said that to this day he prefers to say that his father was ill rather than say he committed suicide.

There is a relationship between the manner in which society views suicide and the way it is viewed in the family, even in cases where the family is not ashamed of the act and finds no need to hide the facts. Maya was twelve when her mother committed suicide after many years of mental illness. She said: "My mother prepared me for this. It is an illness; there is nothing to be ashamed of. Now my uncle says, 'You do not have to tell your boyfriend the whole truth'... I was shocked. I am not ashamed of her, and I have never made any effort to hide it.."

In many cases when there is some doubt as to whether it was an accident, family members will continue to uphold the argument that it was. This is an important coping mechanism for the family.

Yehonatan Gefen, an Israeli writer, dedicated his book *Dear Lady*[42] to his mother who committed suicide. He said that all his mother's closest friends insisted that his mother had not committed suicide but had, by mistake, taken one pill too many.

A high emotional price is often paid for hiding the truth about a suicide and transforming it into a secret. The amount of energy invested in keeping the secret, may harm rather than help the family. Revelation of the secret allows for a new relationship with the narrative and for closer contact between the various family members. The question is, can one talk to anyone about the suicide? If one dares to speak of it within the family can one also speak of it with others? Leonora's mother committed suicide when Leonora was in the army. She understood from her father that she was able to discuss it with friends, but just the closest ones, certainly not with anyone. There is a question as to whom the story of the suicide 'belongs'. For some family members it is taboo. If the truth about the suicide is revealed, other family members may be exposed against their will. They may not be prepared for this exposure.

This was my experience when I was interviewed by a news reporter. As my mission is to emphasize that suicide it a topic that should be discussed free of shame I was well aware that the article would feature my name, and since one should not to be ashamed, why then remain anonymous? However the article exposed other members of my family who had not been through the same process I had, and for them the exposure was problematic. I wanted to prepare my extended family for the public exposure which was to be expected following the publication. When I told my aunt, my father's sister, that there was going to be an article about my research in a newspaper she was very

---

42 Yehonatan Gefen, *Dear Lady*. Tel Aviv: Dvir, 1999

angry. "Do you want people to know?" It is thirty years after his suicide, and since she does not talk about it she still thinks other people don't know the true story of his death!

Susan, one of my interviewees, recalls how angry she was with her husband when he told their daughter of her grandparents' suicide, not because he had talked about it, but because she felt it was her story and up to her to decide how, when, and to whom to speak of it.

Arthur (1972)[43] discusses the difficulty of those who were children when their parent committed suicide. The ability of the surviving parent to deal with the suicide, and parents' ability to encourage children to share their emotions is an important factor in determining how children will be able to share their story with others in the future. The suicide does not become a secret in and of itself, but rather becomes one as a result of the child's observations of verbal and non-verbal cues from people around them. In the final analysis, all the surviving family members deal with the difficulties in their own way, however dealing with the suicide alone creates solitude and isolation, and is never simple. It means that there are no means of sharing, or asking for, or receiving help. The absence of accurate information influences the ability to share the pain with others, to speak of it and thereby to find some relief in the process of mourning.

In most cases, as they grow up children need to share their feelings with others. As a result of keeping the secret and hiding the suicide for so many years, they may need to meet others who have had similar experiences, those with whom they can share their thoughts, their questions, their pain, and their fears. Some may feel that not only do they want to help themselves, to obtain relief from the fact that they are not alone, but they also want to help others. They may want to prevent others from experiencing the difficulties that they themselves encountered; they may even feel that they are able to prevent other suicides from occurring. The taboo of disclosure is powerful and this lies not only in the difficulty of being unable to share the facts with others but also in the inability to do so within the family and with those closest. When explaining her willingness to be interviewed Susan told her husband that she could not talk to him about it adding that she wanted to meet me (the author) to verify that she was not alone and that there were others like her with the same fears.

Even in the cases when survivors are able to share and to speak of the

---

43 Arthur, B. (1972). Parent Suicide: a family affair. In: A. C. Cain (Ed.). Survivors of Suicide. 256-260

suicide with others generally it can only be shared with very close friends. It appears that this emanates from an ongoing fear of possible negative responses. The assurance of feeling protected may derive from two sources: being accepted and surrounded by close friends, or being in a situation where others have had the same experience and there is a feeling of 'kinship' rather than rejection and disapproval even once the story has been told. However the possibility of society's stigma still exists. Although revealing the secret does allow the survivor some feeling of resolution and relief about the hitherto hidden story, there is still a price to be paid. The outcome of exposing the truth is not always positive. Perhaps this is the reason that family members choose to reveal their secret in situations where the consequences are less harsh.

The question of how much children continue to be burdened by their childhood difficulties depends on many factors. In an interview with Eilat Negev[44], Nadine Gordimer the Nobel Prize laureate talks about two kinds of people, those who never forget being robbed of their childhood, blaming this for all future flaws in their lives; and those who have learnt to leave it behind and to continue regardless. She says that she belongs to the latter group.

---

44 Negev, E. Private Life. Tel Aviv: Yedioth Achronot

Leonora

My mother committed suicide twenty years ago, when I was twenty. Although on the one hand the suicide itself did not surprise me, I was in a total shock. I mourned her loss for fourteen years. I studied many things and worked in different fields. I reached the top in whatever I did. I think that my desire to be a high achiever probably stems from feeling that my mother was a failure in her life. Today I am a consultant. It's a sterile profession, no warmth, no stress, no suffering. This choice was also influenced by my mother's suicide.

I believe that nothing happens by chance. This belief is confirmed when I look at my own life. My mother was a holocaust survivor. As a child she grew up in a very warm and supportive house. When she was eight or nine the Second World War broke out and all this stability totally collapsed. As she was the oldest child she was separated from her parents and her little sister. Her family was wealthy, well known, and respected. After the war her father died and her mother remarried. I also found out not long ago that her stepfather probably hurt her. Recently I went to Hungary and interviewed my grandmother's sister. She claimed that my grandmother didn't know anything about what her husband was doing to my mother, but her own husband, who was dying at the time (he died one month after my visit), told her in Hungarian not to lie to me.

My mother studied in a Jewish school not far from their home. One morning, during the war, some people from Israel who wanted to try and save children came and took children back with them. The children barely had a chance to say goodbye to their parents. This was the last time my mother saw her parents. Her little sister studied in the local school so she was not taken. My mother was seventeen when she arrived in Israel. She became an Israeli citizen and like so many other European kids who were saved from the holocaust and were brought to Israel, became tough and strong.[45] During her adolescent years she seemed to cope with life reasonably well.

Years later, after my brother was born, she started having problems. My parents were poor, my father was a medical student and she had no relatives nearby. Some members of her family who survived the war came to Israel in 1950 but life was not easy and they left immediately. After that

---

45   (Translator's note: there was a movement called the Youth Immigration Project which was established to bring Jewish youth (without their parents) to Israel to save them from the machinations of the Second World War.

things just became too much for her.

She had her first breakdown when I was four years old. She was later diagnosed as being manic-depressive although to this day I'm not sure that this diagnosis was accurate. It doesn't really matter, the important thing is that from when I was about four until I was twenty, she was in and out of psychiatric hospitals and fluctuated between periods of total isolation completely doped up on pills, to periods when she was a marvellous mother. I always knew what was going on with her but there were people, even her closest friends, who had no idea what went on in our house.

I forgot to mention one very important point – my father is a doctor. Throughout the years he explained to me that my mother was sick, and that her sickness was just like any other sickness. He repeated this throughout my life so that I could understand it at every age. This approach was really helpful for me. Thanks to it I did not suffer from the stigma that mental illness often brings. Often children with parents like my mother bear a heavy load. I didn't. She had periods of total self-confidence and then she'd have a breakdown. The problem was that I didn't know when the next one would appear unexpectedly. My entire childhood I grew up with the feeling that something unexpected could be waiting for me when I opened the door at home. I was afraid to enter my mother's bedroom. Perhaps she'd be dead already. I understood that she could commit suicide at any time; she had made previous attempts although I only found out about some of them later. It has very many implications. But in a way her death itself made it easier for me. It harmed me, and at the same time it strengthened me. In fact I lived all my life in a state of preparedness.

During the last month of her life I had a feeling that something was going on with her. She talked nonsense on the phone and in retrospect she sent out some clear signs. One Friday I was delayed on my way home from the army. I was twenty. When I finally got home I was told that she had committed suicide. I felt the ground sink beneath my feet. Nothing seemed real. But half an hour later I realized that the responsibility of the family was on my shoulders. Both my father and my brother totally collapsed.

It was clear that this time she meant it; this wasn't just a cry for help. She jumped out of a window from a height, unlike the previous attempts which had been cries for help; at those times she had taken pills but had not really risked her life. This time it was clear, she was determined. She left us a letter, which appeared to be very calm, very... sane. In it she asked us to respect her deed. Many years went by until I was able to understand what she had written. She simply said, "Death is better for me than my life, and it is not *against* you, it is *for* me." Generally speaking I respected her request. I figured that if that is what she wanted, that is what I would do. Friends have asked me how I could respect someone's self inflicted death, but I understood that when the will for life is lost, one can become totally desperate. I accepted it as something human and ultimately the suicide act itself was the least important part of the story for me. The terrible part was being a child of a mentally-ill parent. When you have a mentally ill parent you have to pretend all your life. You have to pretend that you are alright. You have to push away the pain and despair, especially in my case where I had to do it all by myself. There were occasions when my mother had a breakdown at home and I had to call the doctors. The problem is that it impedes your growth, your development. I had no one on earth to support me. I remember telling a friend in high school that I decided that my dad was more important to me than my mum. Obviously this is what I decided...

My mother's family never came to see us and they didn't even come to the funeral. I went to visit them in Hungary. I was really furious. When I entered their house I attacked them out of pain and a need for revenge. When her brother came to visit us twenty years later we went to the cemetery together. When he left her grave crying, I said to him "I wonder what she would have said had she known it took you twenty years to come to visit."

Her suicide has created a feeling of revenge within me and I want to take these feelings out on the people who didn't help her when she needed them. I don't blame her for committing suicide, nor for causing me problems throughout my life, but I don't forgive those who were not there for her when she needed them.

I have now lived without her for as many years as I lived with her. That means something to me. From now on I'll have more years without than with. I feel that growing up as a girl with a sick mother as a role model has meant that my mothering instincts have been affected. The most powerful aspect of my growth was survival. In my childhood this meant social survival, I had to be busy all the time, I needed to be popular and have strong ties with friends because I had to hold on to someone, to something. As an adult I always felt that I had to prove myself, and in the past few years I have striven to find inner peace. This is the psychological process I've been going through.

All these years I wasn't bothered by the fact that my mother committed suicide. It is hard for me to separate the suicide act itself from the history of her sickness; in a way her suicide released me. I grew up bearing an enormous load, mentally, emotionally, technically, and family-wise. My problem was with the pain, the loss, and the misery. I was jealous of my girlfriends who had mothers and whose lives were easier than mine. Somewhere in my heart I always knew that she'd commit suicide one day. The problem was with her sudden disappearance. When I saw friends speaking disrespectfully to their mothers I told them that they should appreciate what they have since I had no mother at all.

I treated her sickness as something physiological, in the same way as if someone had cancer and couldn't take it anymore. My mother could not cope with the suffering and the despair. She took her life into her own hands and I see this as a mechanical act. I keep thinking about how desperate a person with kids must be to do something like this. Since I have never been in her position, I can't criticize her. I have had my share of sorrows, but they are those of a healthy person, not a sick one, and there is a big difference between the two. I just felt that it was such a shame, what a pity. This is why I never found it difficult to talk about it. As soon as I made close friends I would tell them everything. I met friends who, at first, thought I was a snob and then when I told them my story they were stunned. I didn't tell just anybody. I felt I needed a certain amount of intimacy in order to talk about it, but today I don't even feel the need for this intimacy. It is just another aspect of my life story.

Her suicide has impacted my life in other ways, for instance I developed a trauma to hospitals so much so that I even found giving birth in a hospital problematic. I had no tolerance for anything depressing or helpless but I think that over the last five years I have finally managed to find a fine balance. I'm really afraid of heights. When my child gets too close to the edge of anything, not just a cliff, I freeze. I can't speak. Because of the way my mother died, anything to do with falling frightens me. What affected me most was the sudden farewell. When someone is ill there is a process of preparation. The sudden farewell has made me constantly fearful of catastrophes. I am always ready for the sky to fall in on me but I know I'll survive.

I believe that I belong to a group of people who share something in their lives which makes them see things, and feel differently. Her suicide made me feel special; it gave me a feeling of uniqueness. It gave me depth and layers which do not exist in other people who haven't experienced this. It gave me understanding of the fabric of life and deep feelings: pain, strengths, and weaknesses. People who have not experienced a disaster such as this don't experience the world as I do. I don't judge them, I just see life differently, think differently, and feel differently. I deeply value people close to me, I value friendship. But I have never questioned how her suicide changed me, never.

One thing that is difficult for me is coping with bureaucracy. To this very day when I'm asked for the cause of death I say she was ill. I tried looking for a formal definition since I thought no one would understand. For years I felt that I was lying but today I feel that this is the real truth; a person who is hospitalized on and off for sixteen years is a sick person. I think that society may want to stigmatize me, either as potentially suicidal, or someone belonging to a high risk group. I was afraid that I might lose some of my National Health fund rights had people known about the suicide.

I would have liked to tell all the kids who have parents like my mother that they don't need to live with a stigma. What saved me was that for my entire life I saw suicide as a disease. I have dreamt of writing a book for adolescents. There was one occasion when someone told me that my mother was crazy, but I had my own beliefs... she was ill and not crazy as she would have been labelled in the Middle Ages. I hate psychiatrists. They drugged my mother. I'm not sure what triggered her decision that morning even though I believe that even with today's medical knowledge there was no way to save her, but perhaps they could have improved her quality of life.

One thing I forgot to mention was the pitying looks I received. I could see in people's eyes that they thought I was a 'poor girl'. This really bothered me but I managed to ignore these looks and I put on a happy face as if nothing bothered me. This was my way of surviving then, my way of not being depressed. A month after her death I started studying at the university. I didn't have time to be miserable, I really wanted to succeed, and the last thing I wanted was to be miserable. If I have any trauma at all it is to do with the physical side of death, the idea of a decaying body. Because of this thought I couldn't attend funerals for years.

I won't tell my children about their grandmother until they are adults, not because I have a problem talking about it, but I don't think they'll be able to understand. I'm apprehensive and afraid that they'll ask questions I can't answer. I'll only tell them when I'm convinced that they won't try to see what it's like. When they ask me how my mother died I say she was ill. I suffered from pain, loss, and loneliness. I pitied myself because I had no mother and had to grow up alone, but I have no problem talking about it. That does not mean that everyone who knows me knows my life story, not at all.

Interviewer: Do you ever think about what would have happened that day had you not been delayed on your way home?

I am sure she would have done it anyway, if not on that day then some other day. Something else would have triggered it. I don't believe that I had any power to change destiny. There was no way to prevent it. I don't have guilt feelings that if I was good girl it wouldn't have happened. It's irrelevant. I only told you that I was delayed in order to point out that while my mother had fallen into her abyss, I was involved my own life. This enabled me to understand that each of us is alone in the world, we live alone, and we die alone, no matter what are we do in between, ultimately we are alone.

I decided that I needed help, and went to therapy. The first therapist I had was awful; he could have easily ruined my life. It took two years until I found another one. I had no problem with the fact that my mother was under psychiatric care and what that meant for me. Through therapy I came to realize that my understanding of motherhood came from my mother and therefore I would not be able to be a perfect mother because I had no proper role model. I don't blame anyone but it was important for me to understand this. Do I have to overcome all my weaknesses? No!

It was also important for me to understand my relationship with my father, the man who always had explanations for everything and then suddenly when it came to it, he completely collapsed. He stopped talking about her, as if she had never existed. He had a friend who helped him a bit, but wasn't smart enough to help my brother and me. There was no one in the world who said here are two lost souls, no one. But I abandoned that place of weakness very quickly.

I discovered something very meaningful for me and perhaps also relevant for research. Even at the worst times I was never afraid that it would happen to me, too. It was always crystal clear to me that I am a healthy person in crisis, and I coped with the crisis positively. A disaster such as this must disrupt your life to a great extent, but I feel strong enough to absorb and process my pain. I never thought that it was out of control. If someone has a parent with cancer they feel that every time they cough they too might have cancer?!

My mother had no chance to recover after what she went through in her life. After going through what she did during the holocaust, and after the way she suffered before she died, dying was much less frightening. I strongly believe that what had caused her sickness was what she went through in her youth.

Interviewer: How is this connected to what you have said of her illness as being physical?

I don't know what came first. I have the feeling that had she received help at the right time she would have coped differently. It is irrelevant. I was angry at the situation, not at her. I don't feel any anger at all towards her. I never felt angry. I can identify with her and understand why living was not an option for her any more.

I am convinced that there is a reason that I have only sons. It's because my feminine, mothering role model was problematic. I feel that I have always identified with my father because the role of a mother was 'sick', and I tended to connect to the strong position. My feminine role modelling is flawed and I think that had I had a daughter it would have been difficult for me to be a good role model for her. The fact that I have sons has enabled me to reveal my weaknesses and not try to be a role model all the time. I have no open wounds anymore. I have a scar – a big one, but I am beyond crying.

Did you cry?

A little. There were many years when it was very difficult for me to talk about losing my mother.

Do you miss her?

Yes, always... Especially when the kids were born. The sadness is always there. I feel sad for her – why did god punish her over and over. And I feel sad for myself. It is a pity that I had such a childhood, and I pay a heavy price for not having a mother. I have no mother to call. Sadness is part of my life, it's already my friend.

I am intimidated by everything that deals with humanity and physicality. That is why I have chosen to work in the arts. I was attracted by the security of artificial beauty, and the fact that everything is predictable. Nothing will suddenly move, the picture will not start walking. I need to be in control yet I can also be weak, but only temporarily. I feel the need to constantly prove that I am valuable. Now, little things mean a lot, things I had no time to concern myself with as I was busy surviving. My life was crazy; I had no time to breathe. Today it is hard for me to remain in a situation I don't like as I had to suffer in a situation like that for so many years. I find it difficult to live a mundane life. Most people just roll along like they're on a wave, but I zig-zag all over the place, turning here and then there.

I never thought I could be a regular person and live just like everyone else. I see things differently. It is important that I am very articulate. Part of my mask is this fluency and my smiling demeanour. I think this makes it appear as if you have no problems. For me this is an integral part of surviving and escaping misery.

I cannot begin to describe the incredible price I have paid for survival. I am on the defense all the time. I will never know the Leonora I once was, and I do feel that loss. The price I have paid is reflected in my life. No words can describe it. I don't feel out of place; on the outside I look tough and unscathed, but on the inside I'm devastated.

MEN AND WOMEN:
SUICIDE AND GENDER DIFFERENCES

A parent who commits suicide when their child is developing as a person, and developing their sexual identity, leaves that child alone at the point of time when the child could learn from, and use, their parent's life experience. The child is suddenly left alone while this significant person (their parent) disappears, leaving the child with no identity figure. The inability to talk about these feelings, exacerbate the child's difficulties in coping with the suicide and its impact. Some factors which have the greatest bearing on the ability to cope with the suicide are: the age of the child when the parent commits suicide, and the gender of both the parent and the child.

Marsha, whose father committed suicide when she was 12 years old, says: "... he ruined my life. For more than 20 years I didn't visit his grave. He ruined my perception of self – who I am as a woman. He robbed me of the feeling that I was wanted or that a man would ever love me..."

Granot [46] claims that when a girl loses her father at an early age, she loses the person who is her first male suitor; the admiration of a father for his daughter is the basis upon which a girl begins to understand her femininity. Indeed Marsha's story demonstrates clearly what happens when this is taken away.

Losing a same-gender-parent also has serious implications for the surviving child. Adam, whose father committed suicide when he was twelve years old, says: "I am angry... he left me without a father. How am I supposed to grow up? I had no one to learn from, so I feel more anger than understanding." Granot further states that when a boy loses his father by suicide, he also loses the male figure with whom he should identify, from

---

46 Granot, T. (2000) Without You: the Impact of Loss and Mourning on Children and Youth .Jerusalem: Publication of the Ministry of Defense.

whom he should learn how to behave and how 'to become a man'. When it is a suicide, the feelings of rejection and abandonment are intensified.

Research of the reactions of people to the loss of their parents under natural circumstances, has found that women tend to have stronger emotional ties with their parents after their parent's death than men do. Women express more pain, and for women a parent's death triggers a cycle of grief for each and every loss in the family. Gender has been found to have a meaningful impact on the way people react to their parents' death.[47]

There are significant differences in the ways men and women experience trauma and difficulties in their lives. In the light of social norms, men are encouraged to distance themselves from intimacy and from those skills and values upon which deep emotional connections are built. Hence, boys 'become men' by suppressing their sensitivity; sometimes men deny being affected by a trauma which may affect them for many years or even for life. Thus boys learn to reject help and comfort during childhood and this may continue, even for life.

Women, on the other hand, tend to share their problems with others and seek help when they feel they need it. This is true also when coping with suicide in their family; in women the process is visible and expression is direct, while men, fearing to expose what they consider to be their weaknesses, express grief by occupying themselves with performing tasks, and attempting to solve problems rather than understanding their source. The very need to seek help is perceived by men as weakness, and in fact they process grief through their various family members.

In the interviews, I found that there were significant differences in the ways men and women described the impact of the suicide on them. Men reported that with the passing of time, the suicide had less impact on them than it did on the women; women claimed that the suicide had a decisive influence on their lives, on their sense of identity, on their personal and professional decisions, etc.

In many cases the male interviewees said that the effect of the suicide was limited, both in its long term ramifications and its impact on their lives as adults. Women, on the other hand, perceived the suicide as an event which reached the core of their very existence, and affected their sense of identity. Susan said: "I carry the feeling of guilt with me everywhere... there are always fears; it's an experience which doesn't leave me; I can't get rid of it. All the

---

47   Moss, Resch and Moss (1997) The Role of Gender in Middle- Age Children Responses to Parent Death. *Omega* 35(1).

time – death lurks just around the corner, somewhere. It is something which remains with you as long as you live."

Michelle talked about her brothers' grief in a similar way: "...my brothers won't talk to you (they wouldn't agree to be interviewed). They have become totally introverted. Men are so scared of showing emotion, or God forbid, crying... when we were preparing the memorial ceremony, my brother asked if he could bring the chairs... anything to avoid being at home, not being close to anything that involved emotions."

David

My father committed suicide when I was twenty-one years old. He had been a farmer all his life. In fact I don't know if he really committed suicide, or whether it was a cry for help. He took pills. This was his second attempt at taking his life. The doctors managed to save his life but he died two days later from a heart attack while he was still in the hospital. I don't really know what the cause of death was, whether it was the pills or the heart attack, but I know he did want to die. It's clear that it was a suicide attempt. He had been depressed for many years. My mother cared for him and we knew that from time to time she would have him admitted to hospital for a short period of time, especially after the Yom Kippur war.

He made his second attempt after my mother died, but he seemed to recover. Then, as a result of various pressures he became depressed again. When he was first admitted to hospital after my mother died it was terrible. I think it was the worst day of my life. For a full day in the hospital they couldn't pinpoint what was wrong with him. Finally they diagnosed the problem and established the correct dose of medication for him to keep him stable. Most of the time he was fine, but when we weren't watching over him he would forget to take his medication and after a couple of weeks he would collapse.

I don't think anything happened to me personally as a result of the suicide. We don't talk about it at home. I think that the difficulties we had with him over the years made it easier to cope with the suicide. He had so few periods of happiness in his life that it hurts me to think about it. It's a little like with a cancer patient; I believe that he was released from his suffering. I don't think that his suicide changed my life. Don't forget I was twenty one years old. I was already mature. It didn't change my direction in life nor any of my decisions. At home we don't speak of the suicide. We remember him, but we don't talk about 'that topic'. I think that he just couldn't go on without my mother. She kept him alive; she was in fact the head of the family. When she passed away her loss had a great impact on us all. We lost young parents. Today I am older than they were when they died. When I see my friends' parents I am so envious. I really miss my parents. The way I work at my job reflects my desire to succeed in everything I do. Perhaps it's because of him, I don't know. But it's clear to me that I want to do everything as well as I can to the best of my ability. 'Suicide' doesn't exist in our house. We don't hide it but we simply don't talk about it. I can imagine what he went through.

We all experience hard times but everyone reacts differently. When times are tough for me I think of him and think that he probably suffered twenty times more than I. He never threatened to kill himself. We have a friend who is always threatening to kill himself. I see this as a warning sign – as a cry for help.

I saw a human being suffers and I understood that he could not bear his situation any longer. I think sometimes a person reaches a point where none of his achievements mean anything to him. Perhaps time changes things. I think today there are far fewer secrets. There is no need to run around and talk about my father's suicide, but my mother for example kept my father's mental condition a secret, even from us. Today we treat mental illness and depression just like any other illness and it needs treatment just like any other illness.

Meryl

I'm twenty seven years old and my father committed suicide four years ago. I'm both working and studying for my second degree at the same time. Until I was nineteen years old we lived in the south of the country where it's fairly quiet, then my parents moved to the center. My father was born in the forests, during the Second World War. He never really knew his father as he was killed when my father was an infant. He never spoke of his childhood and I barely remember my grandmother (his mother) as she passed away when I was a little girl.

Apparently the move to the center of the country triggered his mental breakdown and subsequent suicide. In hindsight everything seems to be connected but the 'official' reason is that he had financial pressures which became too much for him and he was sucked into a whirlpool of despair and financial complications. He had been a huge building contractor during a financial boom . He undertook many projects building complexes which eventually didn't come to fruition and meanwhile he had accrued outstanding debts. He was a self-made man, very successful, and very involved in the community where we lived in the south. Everyone loved and respected him and always came to him for help. I think that part of the reason for the move was to escape the constant pressure on him to help others.

What I do know about his suicide is that he didn't have the strength to deal with the financial difficulties which lay ahead of him. He was expected to give and to give and to give, and he just didn't know how to say no. He left a note which he had written nine months prior to killing himself in which he said he had no more strength, that he felt like a failure, that he was very sorry but he could not go on this way. He had a dream in which he could see the way he wanted his life to be. He planned to quit working at fifty after we, his kids, were all established. Unfortunately the disparity between his dream and the reality was too great.

The family was in total shock. Sometimes people say there was a clue, however in his case we had no idea. On the day he committed suicide, my brother has just graduated, my sister had passed her exams, and we celebrated by having a fun day in Tel Aviv. A friend of the family came to fetch us. He said that there was something wrong with our father but it didn't ring a bell for me. My sister caught on right away that something terrible had happened and became hysterical, but I still didn't realize what was going on. It was a kind of defense mechanism as if I wasn't really there. The drive from Tel Aviv to the house took an hour and the whole way I didn't ask any questions.

As we approached the house my knees went weak, I was afraid and began to cry. But not for a second did I think he was dead, not until we entered our street and I saw the police and an ambulance outside the house. I didn't understand what had happened. Only two hours later did it register that he was dead. I don't remember if I was told in so many words. Until today I still don't know what really happened. I didn't have the guts to ask my brother, who was the one who found him. All I know is that it struck like a thunderbolt out of the blue.

I don't remember what went on at the 'Shiva'. My family is fairly traditional so we observed the customs connected to the Shiva such as not showering or shaving and not changing clothes. There is something very healing in the mourning customs of the Jewish religion. Lots and lots of people came pouring in. It was really a tragedy and when I am at my saddest and when I try to connect to my pain, I miss the Shiva.

My father committed suicide in the city. I don't know the details. There was a gun...I know bits and pieces but I still can't absorb them. We still don't talk about it within the family... not just about 'the event', but about many things. There are many things that have been swept under the carpet. And there are many problems within the family, many problems which have also been swept under the carpet. Our lives changed in a second. The immediate consequence was economic. I believe that no matter how much money I have in my life I'll never feel financially secure.

My mother didn't even have the privilege of grieving. She was thrown straight into a new, very difficult economic reality. She had to fill his place at work and cope with the difficulties of having new problems pop up every day.

The year prior to the suicide had been a very difficult one for me. It was hard for me to decide what to study, what to do with my life... rich people's problems! My father was very important to me. Of all the family members he was the one I was closest to. We really respected one another and I always felt that he had real inner strength. There are times when I really miss him, I'm so sad. Sometimes I feel that if I wish hard enough he might come back. I'm sad because I'm not sure that he understood how much I loved him. If I could talk to him and tell him all the things I never got a chance to say, that would make my pain easier to bear.

The fact that I had problems during the year before he died worried him a lot. He would try to understand what was missing in my life, and he would try to help. How I wish I could talk to him, to explain and justify why I came to him with my problems when he was having such a hard time coping. I think the idea of suicide was brewing in his mind for quite a while and for nine months he carried the suicide note around in his pocket, every day. It's very hard for me to imagine that. For a long time I couldn't understand how hard it was for him, how much he suffered, I thought just of myself. Now I look differently at the people who knew my father.

There are positive aspects to the way the suicide impacted on me. I can connect with my pain and understand other people's pain. Today I know what real pain is and I am able to forgive more easily. I guess these are the good things.

But there are plenty of bad things; suicide is like a black hole. All one's energies are sucked into it and one's reality totally changes. My personal experience has completely changed me. I am a different person today. There is no continuum between 'before' and 'after'. It's me, I'm still me, but my experience has changed me and the way I think and feel. I feel that my choices are influenced by my loss. Even my academic choice to study psychology was not made with the beauty of life in mind. I work with high-risk children and this work puts perspective in my life. Even though I don't discuss it, I don't think it's a coincidence that the children ask me where my father is.

I can't pinpoint exactly how the suicide, as opposed to other things, has changed me but from my point of view everything changed because of the suicide.

The family is a very painful link in this story. My mother completely lost contact with all her friends in the south where we lived in a small community and everyone knew everything about everyone. We thought she would be better off if she moved to the center of the country. The anonymity of a big city suits her very well even though sometimes I think she's running away from life.

I went for therapy and the therapist told me that I was coping really well. She didn't see the price I paid for this façade of 'coping well'. My father also coped... I cope but I am constantly paying a heavy price. It's called faking. There's no point trying to build me up, I have no time for myself. In the past four years I haven't had time to breathe, between work and studies I have no time for myself.

Recently a group of close friends got together. At first I didn't understand what held them together but then I discovered that what bound them was loss. I joined the group and each one had to talk about something very significant in their lives. When they said 'very significant' I immediately thought of the 'Shiva' and I couldn't speak. Four years have passed. This last year has been the most difficult; actually every year has been more difficult than the last. The second was more difficult than the first.

I thought about what would have happened if only... I don't pity myself, I'm not bitter and I don't spend time blaming either my father or myself. In a sense I feel good that he was my father, that he was strong. I would have hated for him to collapse. This way he maintained his self-respect. He always gave to others and when he could give no more he felt that there was no point to his life. He couldn't just 'exist'. But he didn't understand that he had more to give than just money. Today I understand that there were signs, hints, but I can only see them in hindsight.

On the one hand it would have been easier for us had it been an accident and not something he did to himself. On the other hand I feel that he made his own choice and he isn't suffering any more. But then again I think what sort of a choice was that? Is that really a choice? Perhaps he regretted his decision at the last minute, but by then it was too late? When someone is sick, the family gets the opportunity to say goodbye. In this case it was an amputation. Something remains unresolved forever. The most difficult thing for me is that I wasn't able to say goodbye. I place a picture of him on my table and I see that he has worry lines... these drive me crazy. I often try to smooth them out, smooth them out in the picture. To this day I can't and won't say the word 'suicide'. I call it 'the incident' or 'the trauma'.

I tried to function as well as I could but I gained a lot of weight. I guess that's a sign of not functioning very well. The idea of 'the black hole' comes up quite often. I feel all my energy being sucked into it and I feel wrung out. It's as if part of me is missing. I have many resources and abilities to function but part of my energy remains there. I feel like there's a whirlpool and I'm struggling so I won't get sucked into it. My perspective and concept of reality is measured in terms of that darkness. Perhaps it's just an excuse. Does everything have to be put in terms of 'the suicide'? But if that's how I see things then that's how they are. There's something about this tragedy that is very fixating. Emotionally, I can't move on from there.

My mother isn't coping. They were really in love, they were the ideal couple. They always kissed when he came home from work. I remember them kissing. Our home was always filled with love and warmth. My mother says that until his last day he made her blush. I feel that my father was the shepherd of the family and now the flock has scattered. My mother has not been able to separate from him. It's as if she's annoyed and therefore won't speak to him. Yet I don't think she has the energy to separate from him.

The feeling that the suicide was perhaps punishment for something I did has been raised in my therapy. I have had many conversations with God about ethics and morality but I don't think it was a punishment.

When I think of pain I think of my father. Anything painful leads me there, to the black hole.

A DATE WITH DESTINY?

Apart from questions that arise about familial, or even genetic aspects of suicide, and concerns in general about 'suicidality', which is a mysterious, frightening, and threatening phenomenon, there are other questions raised in the family which are also related to the age at the death of the person who committed suicide. Upon reaching that specific age, did something previously dormant, suddenly erupt? And if so, are the offspring also at risk? Could the same trigger cause them to contemplate suicide at the same age? Parents who have had one of their children commit suicide also spoke of the fear that when their younger children reach the same age, they too might be affected by this trigger. These thoughts create concern about reaching 'that same age' at which the person committed suicide, and at the same time – feelings of relief, when the survivors pass this age.

The recurring expressing amongst survivors of the fear that there is an 'age of death' shows that the survivors believe that there are external forces beyond their control. They believe that these forces had an impact on the decision of the deceased to commit suicide and that these forces might, in due course, have the same influence on other family members, or even on themselves. The feelings that one might be controlled by forces which may influence decision-making, is a frightening experience.

Fear of reaching the age at which a parent died even if under other circumstances such as accident, or illness, and not necessarily suicide, also exists in people whose parents died when they were young. Death, under any circumstances, of a parent when a child is young, leaves children feeling that this is a 'dangerous age', and wondering whether they are at risk when they reach the same age.

In her book Motherless Daughters [48] Hope Edelman, who interviewed

---

48   Hope Edelman (1997) *Motherless Daughters*.

women who lost their mothers, at different ages and under varying circumstances, notes that more than three quarters of her interviewees said that they fear that they too might die under similar circumstances. Two thirds of the women under the age of fifty five feared reaching the age that their mothers were at their death. Edelman pointed out that it was interesting that they did not mention fear of dying, but rather fear of dying young. She claims that the same-gender parent functions as a protective barrier between the child and death; when this barrier disappears, death suddenly seems closer and more tangible, and the child has no physical role model to mirror their own aging.

On the other hand, there is relief when the child passes this age, as if the "risk factor" has disappeared: "... I remember that passing the age of forty two – his age when he committed suicide – was a significant event for me; I just had to get past 42 safely. I was so relieved", said Ron.

In many cases these families live according to a unique calendar, before and after the suicide. According to this calendar certain years, and ages, hold unique significance. Marsha, whose father committed suicide at the age of thirty five, relates that she and her brother had "... a 35 year old crisis, not the usual 40 year old crisis." And then there's Leonora who counts the passing years, and tells me that this year will mark to the 20th anniversary of her mother's suicide, when she herself was 20; so from this point on she will have lived more 'without' her, than 'with'.

Marsha

Marsha and her family immigrated to Israel after her father, a doctor, committed suicide. Although her family subsequently left Israel, Marsha stayed and built her life, and a new family there. The researchers Sonneck and Wagner published an article "Suicide and Burnout of Physicians.49 Here they noted that despite the known risk factors for stress and illness among physicians, there is a 'conspiracy of silence' about suicide. Suicide rates among physicians are relatively high, up to six times more than the regular population. They added that the main reasons for suicide among physicians are addiction and depression.

My father committed suicide when I was twelve. It was a few weeks after my birthday. Today I am married and the mother of two, have a Master's degree, and a good job. My father was a successful doctor. My mother had been a housewife, but took a job a year or two before he killed himself. He was addicted, for a few years, he was not on drugs, but to prescription drugs as he was able to write himself prescriptions. The addiction began about five years before he killed himself. He went for therapy but it didn't work for him.

He had a difficult childhood. It seems that his mother was insane, and his father was quiet, reserved. I don't know much more about his childhood.

For a while he was conscripted into the army and was sent to a place where he had less opportunity to self-medicate. When he returned from the army his condition deteriorated. I was ten years old... my mother told me that he was drugged but I didn't really understand. He attempted suicide a couple of times. He crashed into tree and was then hospitalized in a psychiatric ward. After that he improved a little. He came home after his hospitalization and I remember going on a family holiday and feeling that he was better. About two weeks later he committed suicide. He was gone a couple of days and was found in a hotel in another state in the United States. It was clear that he thought he would not be found. This was just before I was to go to a brand new school. This all happened during the summer vacation.

My mother told me that he did not kill himself, and I remember the feeling of relief, which of course meant that I must have known that there was a chance that he had committed suicide. A year later she told us the truth. She was very angry but didn't want us to hear the truth from someone else. I think it took a few years before what she said sank in. Until then I heard, but

---

49   Sonneck, G. & Wagner, R. (1996) Suicide and Burnout of Physicians. Omega(33) 253-263.

suppressed it. It just didn't sink in.

There are many ramifications surrounding suicide. There is the secret itself. My mother kept the cause of death a secret for a long time. My grandfather took on the financial commitments of our family but even some of the immediate family didn't know. My uncle, my mother's brother, knew, but even his wife did not know, and it was clear that it was to be kept that way. I had a friend in high school who said that his father was killed when he fell off a ladder, and I always wondered if that was really the true cause of his death. My father was thirty-five years old when he died. Over the years, the lie became more and more complicated, but I do not remember it weighing heavily on me until I was older. At twenty I became friends with a young woman who today is my very close friend. I told her the truth about my father's death. My mother was so angry with me that she threatened to disown me, claiming that I had betrayed her and the family. To this day when people ask me how my father died it's really difficult for me. It's not that I'm afraid to tell, but the question is, to whom, how, when, where, what to say...

At a certain age I decided that it was *my* story and it was my right to deal with his death as I see fit and not the way my mother wants me to. The secret for me is a matter of principle ... it was hard for me. I decided that I would not keep it a secret. There was nothing for me to hide.

I was always afraid that my parents would die before me and they assured me it would not happen. It is important for me that my children feel secure and safe and are not afraid that their parents will die. I haven't told them about my father yet. I feel that I have to stay alive at least until my daughter is independent. Parents have to be around as long as their children need them... this is important to me.

When my children will begin to show an interest in my father's death, I'll tell them. Why is it a secret? I don't know. But I know that I can't lie about it. I think my mother hid her story because she wanted to protect us, and perhaps she felt she was partly responsible for his suicide. She realized that the pills had disappeared and she didn't do anything to prevent him 'doing it'.

He hugged her and left, and then during the day she saw the pills were gone. It was her secret and then I became an accomplice after she had told me. We went through some tough times in our family. Actually I feel proud that I am who I am, a good person, after all that I went through.

I do not know why I kept the circumstances of his death a secret. Today discussion of suicide is much more open. We don't speak about him with some of our family members. I 'm not even sure if they know. I feel that I should keep it that way. My husband's family does not know about the suicide, not that I'm ashamed, but there seems to be no reason to tell them. If they asked - I don't know what I'd do. My husband of course knows... So maybe I am still keeping it a secret. I think you tell special people something like this, people with whom you have an intimate relationship. If you really respect someone then it's no secret. I tell people who won't be shocked by the story. Each time I repeat it, it's a kind of test of confidence, checking how the listener will respond. At 12 you don't share everything that's happening to you. I don't know why my siblings and I didn't share with each other, help each other. I guess when you're 12 you just don't! This is not an event that was part of the interactions I had with my friends at age twelve. We believed that my mother would protect us from the world. We were locked in a universe of our own about what happened with my father. Later on in life we did talk about it.

It feels like you've been struck by tragedy twice, once because of the death, and a second time because the reason is suicide. This is largely because of the attitude of our society.

When I thought about how to move on and make a success of my life, I felt that he ruined my life. I didn't visit his grave for about 20 years. He didn't deserve it. Last year I took my husband. My mother wanted to come, but I asked her not to come with us. For my husband the visit to the cemetery was very significant as he had never been to the grave with me before.

What does this say about me? How do I go on? How can I be the daughter of a man who should have admired and loved me and how did his suicide affect my relationships with men. I was angry that he was so destructive and left me a flawed legacy regarding my identity as a woman.

When I started therapy I believed that me reaching puberty was problematic for my father; that it was so unbearable for him that he took an overdose of pills. It seemed that my sexual development made him feel he couldn't cope, didn't want to, and felt that suicide was his answer. I felt that my approaching womanhood was significant, and he left. Of course I see all this in hindsight. He never made me feel beautiful and desirable, or that a man could love me. I can't forgive him for this, and I am even angrier over this than over the tangible things, and the fact that he left my mother alone. How could he do that? I felt totally rejected. I really hope that I didn't choose my husband just because I was afraid that I wasn't worthy of anyone else's love. But I can't only blame my father for this. Even though I went to therapy for a number of years I'm not sure that it really helped me, although I hope it did. My father was the love of my mother's life and she never formed a relationship with anyone after his death. In fact she's never had a significant relationship since then. His love made her blossom, and then he killed himself.

Heredity frightens me. There have been many disturbed individuals in our extended family, one of my cousins, my father's brother...although none of them were institutionalized. My grandmother was crazy; my father was depressed when he committed suicide. We have defective genes in our family, and I just hope that we are all sane. Actually I remember that when I was a child he was very accessible to us, quiet and nurturing. But I also remember that when he began to deteriorate, I had a sense of foreboding for a number of years. Once when I came home from school he came down the stairs without even noticing me. I remember feeling frightened that something terrible was about to happen. On one occasion when he wanted to go somewhere by himself, my mother sent me off with him to make sure that he didn't "do anything to himself", or that he wouldn't buy drugs. I remember shaking. He drove really fast and I felt as if we were losing control. I asked him to stop. When I got home I burst into tears and couldn't stop crying. To this day I can't understand how my mother could put this on me. I don't remember feeling any financial pressures or decline in our standard of living. But I do remember being afraid of death. His suicide caused my mother serious problems. There were times when she just walked away and when I asked her "Where are you going?" she would answer, "I don't know." For children, to see their mother come and go like this was disturbing and frightening. It was a torture.

At thirty five years old she was left with three children. Today, now that I myself am a mother I see her as a so brave, a lioness... She has needed a tremendous amount of internal strength to deal with what life did to her. And we paid a high price. As a result of his suicide, her life revolved entirely around us.

We'll never really know what his suicide did to her self-image. For me, reaching the age of thirty-five was a milestone – can one go on living after this age? When I turned thirty-five I had a real anxiety attack, a crisis... I saw life as extremely fragile, and felt that I couldn't guarantee my children a happy life. I connect this anxiety to my father and to the idea that thirty-five is a fatal age. We all felt the significance of this age... not forty which is the usual 'crisis' age.

While I was in therapy there were a few times when I felt that I had to fight the same urge to also do it, but then I felt that I had to tell him that 'this part of you will not infuence me'. Then it disappeared.

FEARS AND COPING

A fter the death of a loved one to suicide, survivors experience anxieties and live with many fears as a result of this tragedy. One of the fears they anticipate and then must cope with is when they themselves reach the age at which their loved one committed suicide, and what this means in terms of their own lives. Other fears such as fear of heights, anxiety that something might happen to their children, and the fear of not being able to control external events, are just a few fears that are common to suicide survivors. The common denominator is that they are all fears of events over which the survivors feel they have no control and yet which would have an impact on their lives.

In cases where suicide threats were made throughout childhood, the fear held by the child was their inability to prevent or change the course of events; this was ultimately confirmed when the suicide occurred. These fears may therefore start when the parent is still alive. This has a crucial effect on their lives both at the time it occurs, and in the future. In her interview Susan reported that her father would repeatedly say that he was going to kill himself. As an adult, her current fears are of climbing and of high places and "... if my children climb on anything high, I have an anxiety attack."

Childhood is the time when parents should provide the most stability; however when this is absent the childhood experience is tenuous, at best. Children live with apprehension and fear as to what to anticipate when opening the door to their home; they are always on the alert for the possibility of returning home to a disaster. All these fears stem from the event over which a child had no control. Thus suicide survivors search for a way to regain control over their lives, control they feel they were denied following the suicide, and in some cases even before it. Suicide survivors have many ways in which they try to overcome these fears. They talk about the need to constantly keep themselves busy, live past 'the age of death', and create successful families and careers. Success reflects stability which is unlike their own childhood and adolescent experience.

Leonora talked about her need to prove herself by excelling in everything she did. She felt that this drive to achieve stemmed from the failure she saw in her mother's life. First and foremost she wanted to prove that her life meant something, was significant; she was almost obsessed with creating a stable life and stable marriage. Roz too, talked about 'chalking up successes'.

In his research, Albert Cain also found that suicide survivors tended to be overachievers and often talking about an overwhelming need to succeed. He claims that this reflects a psychological need to prove how misguided the parent was in choosing not to live and see their child grow up.[50] The same phenomenon may be seen as an expression of an existential need in the child to regain control over his or her life, control which was snatched away by the parent's suicide. This presents a somewhat paradoxical situation. The parent may have made the decision to commit suicide in order to gain control over his very existence to cope and control situations, which he felt he could not otherwise control. However, the outcome of this very deed, results in the feeling of loss of control of his or her own life, by the child. It is this very control that the child is trying to reclaim.

The need for success and stability in adult life, especially career and family, may reflect the need to regain acceptance from the society which rejected the survivors and cast a stigma upon them. Achievements may earn them recognition and respect from this very society from which they feel rejected. In some cultures a person who commits suicide is buried outside the boundaries of the regular cemetery or burial ground. If the person, actually or metaphorically, is cast out of society, the survivor may feel that success and stability reflect a way of integrating back into 'normal' social circles.

The interviewees often felt that they had to work harder and be outstanding when building a career and family since they started out with a disadvantage. Any achievement is perceived as a milestone in overcoming the impact of their parent's suicide on their lives. When Israeli actor, director, and poet Yossi Yizraeli was 21, his father committed suicide. This occurred one month after Yossi completed his compulsory military service. In an interview when asked about his success he stated: "... the enigma of suicide confused and distressed me ... What I have achieved in my life can be summarized by

50 Cain, A. C. (Ed). (1972)

saying that while running forward I am both chasing something and running away, a bit like driving a car and looking in the rearview mirror."[51]

However, the burning desire to succeed, and to keep busy all the time, may not necessarily be perceived as the survivors' victory over the implications of the suicide, but rather as the price they pay. The overwhelming drive to succeed and keep busy is perceived by the survivors as something the suicide has driven them to, rather than an achievement they have attained and chosen freely. They feel that this is actually the only possible alternative for them, that they have no choice.

This serves to reinforce the feeling of lack of control. Ultimately their achievements embody a negative aspect which is sometimes intolerable. Leonora uses harsh words to describe what it takes to function and the price paid: "There are no words to explain what I paid for survival. The price is one's life," she exclaimed. She overcame the impact of living with a mentally-ill mother and as an adult she lives a full and meaningful life. But her life has been forever altered and can never be what it might have been under different circumstances. As she had put it, "The price is life itself."

---

[51] Karpel, D. *Late lust.* Haaretz, 24.10.2003

Joe

I am thirty-one. My father committed suicide when I was twenty-two. At the time I had not made any decisions about my future. His suicide had a huge impact on my whole life. I think that the age you are at the time of the tragedy is very important in the way it impacts on you at the time, and in the future. As a result of his suicide I developed many problems. It affected my self-confidence and my self-esteem, and as a result, I started having problems at work. To this day I am still affected by the impact of his suicide. I am sure everyone in the family is affected differently. Had it not happened to me, I am sure my life would have looked completely different irrespective of the kind of relationship I had with my father; I crave having a father, now and forever. I lived at home until six months ago. I felt that I needed to stay with my mother, to look after her and protect her.

I assume that the idea of suicide occurs to everyone at one time or another. But one should be able to overcome a weak moment. He did it in the house, in his room, and my little sister found him. When I came home, the street was full of police. I didn't understand what happened... and then I simply lost control! I started screaming, "Couldn't you save him?"

For several months I couldn't accept that he was dead. I had vivid dreams about him; I had visions of him coming home. The whole family misses him... mostly on the holidays. There is no way of filling the void.

If this disaster taught me anything it is that a person should never be too proud to accept help or to share. The price of pride is disaster. In our home, we were all too proud to share our troubles. It wasn't the 'honorable' thing to do. No self-respecting adult would admit that they had a problem. Because he was such a proud person no one thought to ask my father how he was or if he needed help, even though there was a sense that something was wrong. There were signs... not signs that he was going to kill himself. He would isolate himself in his room, but we never checked his room or his things. We didn't think we should check what was going on there.

For a long time after it happened I found it hard to hold down a steady job. Only now I am starting to feel that I am moving ahead and may have overcome the crisis. I'm glad I went to therapy; I don't feel that I need to feel ashamed. I don't feel that therapy changed the way I live my life but it helped me cope with the grief.

Of course there were economic implications. My mother became the sole provider. I often wonder why people do not talk about suicide, not only in my family but in general. It's a sensitive topic. In the army, for example, anyone could commit suicide; often no one really picks up on the cues. When I served in the army and had a crisis no one was even aware of my mental state. The army tends to help people who are proactive in seeking assistance. I think it is important to prevent more incidents of suicide in the future.

I don't tell my story to everyone. When I do talk about the suicide I don't deny it or say that my father had cancer or anything like that, but I only talk about it with close friends.

A good friend of mine insists that I underestimate the impact of suicide on myself. She says that I am actually quite traumatized. I told her that one usually hears about happy families, and that I have a different story. I feel that I am different than other people. I know I could do more with my life. I could have gone to university, but because of these difficulties and my lack of self-confidence, I didn't study. I am sure that it changed the course of my life. Because of the suicide I don't do things I dreamt of doing, I have dreams I know I won't fulfill – it's too late!

I would like to meet other people who have had the same tragic experience. I think meeting other people who have experienced loss through suicide would give me a feeling of identification, a feeling that I am not the only one with these problems. Now the most important thing for me is to talk about the suicide, and meet other people like myself. I think suicide survivors need a place to meet each other. People are ashamed to get treatment, but an opportunity to meet may help them cope with the ongoing effects of suicide. There also should be more public awareness of the suffering that suicide creates in the survivors.

I am not angry with my father. I understand that he must have suffered, and that he felt he had no other option. It is important for me to feel positive about him.

My father's suicide has created many problems for me, but at the same time it has made me a more open person, because I have seen what happens when people don't talk about their problems, and don't know how to deal with them.

PARENTAL ROLES

In a child's life each parent fulfills many roles such as providing education, influencing their identity, caring for their mental and physical needs, providing food and clothing, protecting them from danger, and nurturing them. During childhood and adolescence parents provide the tools so their children can grow up to become productive and functioning adults. A parent who commits suicide leaves his children in a vacuum with no role model and no one to fulfill these roles. Parental roles vary according to the age of the children. Therefore, the age of the child when a parent commits suicide, is significant. This is also true regardless of the circumstances of the loss of a parent, but suicide intensifies the loss and the implications of this loss.

The death of a parent, no matter what the reason, creates a void in the child's life and the parental roles disappear, and the child's need for the parent is no longer met. When talking about parental roles there are multi-faceted implications for survivors. There is the feeling that the parent failed to fulfill their obligation. This feeling may be retrospective.

The child may have felt the lack of parenting while the parent was still alive. For example in cases where the parent suffered from some form of mental illness, this obviously affected the way in which the parent functioned throughout the child's life prior to the suicide.

Some children are forced to take on the role of a parent both with a parent who cannot function, and after a parent's death, when the surviving parent finds it difficult to fulfill the roles of both parents. In these cases parents sometimes ask the children, particularly the older ones (even when they may still be very young), for daily assistance in running the household.

As the surviving children grow up they often feel that the model set by their (deceased) parent will have an impact on their own parenting. When a parent commits suicide it changes the assumed natural role and order in life which is that parents will always be there to protect their children. When a parent commits suicide, the unspoken promise of parental protection disappears. The child feels vulnerable now that the protective umbrella of the parent has gone. If something as unbearable as this event took place, what assurance can one give a child that it cannot happen to the other parent too? Marsha refers to this when she talks about her worst nightmare - the hidden threat that her mother, too, may disappear.

Children learn basic behavioral codes from their parents. These codes are needed to develop their own identity and values, and it is from their parents that they learn to cope both in times of joy and sorrow. This is denied the child whose parent commits suicide. Children often only realize or become aware of how important their parents are to them after the parent is gone. Adam asks: "Who am I supposed to learn from now?" He realizes just how many things his father could have taught him, but now he has been robbed of the opportunity and he finds himself alone. His solution is to seek other male company for 'man to man' talks; but it is clear to him that this is not an adequate substitute.

When the parental role model disappears children often adopt the parental role, fully or partially. Sometimes it is about the missing breadwinner and sometimes it is about simply being the head of the family. Ron, who lost his father when he was fourteen, states that "we went on with our lives, but it was without him. I started working in the family farm. As I was the oldest son, the responsibility lay on my shoulders, and it was a heavy responsibility to bear. I became the head of the family."

Sometimes the role of 'family carer' is taken on by the children (sometimes very young ones) even while the parent is still alive. This is true especially in cases where a parent has a history of mentally illness and at times when the parent cannot function adequately. The role is not necessary given to the child by the other parent, but is simply adopted by children themselves. Maya, who grew up in a single parent home with her mentally-ill mother, says: "When her mental condition really deteriorated I had to hospitalize her. I was seven or eight years old at the time."

It is almost impossible to imagine: what goes through a child's mind, when at the age of seven or eight, or even 'at the ripe old age' of fourteen, they ought to take responsibility for a parent, involving caring, hospitalizing, or trying to prevent them from carrying out their threat to commit suicide? How does a child grapple with the complex tasks that the circumstance of his life, or the other parent, has foisted upon him? From the interviews it is clear that children take these roles upon themselves often without questioning, even though this role robs them of the life enjoyed by their peers. The term used by family therapists for these children is 'parental children'.

The feeling that the parental role was not fulfilled by their own parent projects directly on the survivors, leaving them questioning their own ability to function both as adults, and as parents themselves. With the act of suicide the parent leaves an indelible mark on the child and the impact lives on long after the suicide. Even as grown-ups and in parenthood, there is no escape from the memories and the effect these have on their own parenting. Susan questions her ability and asks "how can I avoid repeating their mistakes…" She wonders how she can encourage her children to speak and share freely and openly with her. Someone who has lost a parent to suicide is unable to model themselves on their parents' behavior. Under regular circumstances one asks oneself how their own parent would behave in a particular situation; however survivors must create a new parenting model, as they have no role model and no helpful childhood memories from which to draw. There is the added physical perspective. The child cannot imagine the deceased parent growing old. The child becomes older than the age the parent was when he committed suicide, the difference being that the child lives on. From now on the parent will remain forever young, and the maturing children will no longer have the path of their parents to emulate.

Ron

I am 44 years old. When I was 14 years old and in 8th grade my father, who was a farmer, committed suicide. I had no idea that he was at all troubled before he did it, nor did I have any idea about the actual suicide itself. He had tried to kill himself the year before, when I was in 7th grade; we (his children) also had no idea about the attempted suicide. He took an overdose, but at the last minute he was saved in hospital.

On the day that he 'succeeded', he simply didn't come home. He went out to work in the fields and didn't come home. My mother sent me out to the fields to see why he was late home for lunch. I took my bike and started looking for him, I called out for him, and then I saw him lying face down on the ground. I turned him over and immediately realized that he was dead, even though as a kid of fourteen I didn't quite understand what had happened. Only in hindsight, did I really understand.

I called out to other people who were working in the neighboring fields and they took him to the hospital. After an hour or two my mother returned from the hospital and told us that he had died. We had no idea that he had committed suicide. I had never heard the word 'suicide' in our household. It wasn't anything that we had talked about. We were told that he had been bitten by a snake. My mother never mentioned the suicide; she never told us that he had committed suicide. In fact everyone tried to suppress his memory for all of us.

We sat "Shiva". The house was full of people all the time. Then our lives went on without him. I started to run the farm, the orchards and the cowsheds. It's difficult for me to describe how this all affected my life. Obviously it had an impact on my life and was an enormous change. I was 14, the eldest child, and was suddenly responsible for my mother and my younger siblings. The role naturally made me mature quickly, and I felt 'old', I felt as if I was a responsible adult, the head of the family.

My father studied his whole life. I imagine that he felt extremely frustrated at the gap between his potential, and what he was actually doing with his life. It's difficult for me to say how the suicide affected my life. It left its mark, I matured prematurely; I had a different way of looking at things, and suddenly I was totally in another place. But it wasn't that I suddenly became introverted or acted differently. I did have a happy childhood.

When I was in the army I met a girl whose father had also died at an early age, and we spoke about the fact that these circumstances mature you and give you a totally different outlook on life. The trauma is still a trauma, but I'm not sure whether the suicide affected the direction my life has taken, or the choices I have made.

Only years later was I told that he committed suicide. My girlfriend was the one who told me. She said it in an offhand kind of way, as in "by the way... you know that they say he committed suicide..." I think that when she told me she was sure that I knew.

I was really shocked, but immediately realized that it was true. There are things that you intuitively know are true. Suddenly things fell into place. Only in recent years have I heard the whole story from my mother. But I really believe that I am emotionally healthy; the suicide did not damage me forever. I lived through the loss, and the pain it caused was not irreversible. That's how I describe it.

The only problem I have is when people ask me how my father died. The answer gets stuck in my throat, and I can't get it out. I tell people that he was sick...I can't get 'that word' out of my mouth...and I get asked quite often, so either I ignore the question, or I change the subject. Today I am older than he was when he died. It's hard for me to talk about it because no one ever talked to me about it, or about him. Talking about him in any way was allegedly taboo. It's not an easy situation. But apart from the difficulty of saying he committed suicide, I don't feel that I have any problems that need solving. Perhaps he exists somewhere...

I guess my mother had no one to talk to about the suicide, and so it was very difficult for her to talk to us about it. She coped with everything on her own. At that time, people didn't know how to help her, and no one felt the need, or knew how, to offer any assistance. I assume, or at least hope, that nowadays situations like ours, where a family has nowhere to turn, just don't exist anymore.

We don't have commemorations for him, and we don't visit his grave. Memories are not measured by those things, but it seems that any memory of him has been erased from our family history, from our memory and consciousness. I do remember what he looked like, after all I did spend many years of my life with him, but the memory of him as a person has been erased. As a father he has disappeared. If a topic isn't talked about at home, a child doesn't raise it. The date of his death means nothing to me. We don't do anything to commemorate his memory, and I think this is a mistake. We only go to his grave if we happen to be at the cemetery for something else. At first, the family was afraid to tell us that our father had committed suicide; I guess this was to protect us from the trauma and perhaps from the stigma.

Then, as time went by they probably thought why should we talk about it now? And then, in time, I guess it became irrelevant. From the decision not to tell us that he committed suicide, we got to the situation where no one spoke about him at all, and it seemed that all memory of him would disappear.

I have no idea why he committed suicide. That's the only thing that bothers me and I think about it. The answer I tell myself is that he had a personality flaw which wasn't dealt with properly. It seems he lived with internal confusion, fighting and conflicted within himself about what he thought he could do, and what he was actually doing. He strove for excellence and his daily life held him back. I believe that this is what finally drove him to commit suicide, but I can't be sure. I think a lot about whether it's hereditary. It bothers me. I really hope that something like this never happen again in our family. But it's definitely an option that exists in my mind. I also hope that we would know how to help anyone who is experiencing any similar kind of difficulties.

I remember that I always thought that it was important to get past the age of 42, the age he was when he committed suicide, it was a milestone. I told myself that I had to get past that age safely. Perhaps it kicks in at 42? Perhaps there's a hidden, latent gene that emerges. In fact I really felt a sense of relief when I reached and passed the age of 42.

One way in which his suicide really did affect me is the total sense of responsibility I feel for my whole family. Emotionality and responsibility have accompanied me ever since. I believe that it's important to prevent emotional anguish and help whenever and wherever possible so something like this never happens again.

So often I think what a pity this happened. After all, my life could have been quite different. I grew up without a father. It's such a shame that he never knew his grandchildren, my children, and in fact he barely knew me. His disappearance from my life made my life more difficult, but the difficulties actually influenced my choices and my development. Life went on, it just went on differently, but it went on.

Guilt was never something I felt, and I don't believe there is even a basis for any guilt. I don't feel as if there is anything left unresolved. It's an experience which will stay with me for my whole life but at some point there has been a closure.

I would have loved to ask him all sorts of questions. I would be happy if he appeared suddenly in my dreams. I think he had lots to give me. He had lots of knowledge and wisdom and it would have been great to share it. I would like to ask him questions to help me understand why he did it, at least to try to understand.

For a long time I tried to avoid talking about the suicide. Perhaps I was afraid that talking would open up the wounds. I don't know why I didn't talk about it sooner...it's part of my heritage, it's my life, and it's important to talk about things like this. We always have to remember that it's in our hands. It's important to talk and prevent things like this from happening in the future.

Maya

I am 24 years old. I'm completing my Masters Degree, have a job, and I live with my boyfriend.

My mother was a single parent. When I was born I think she may have been hospitalized in a mental institution; if not, she was certainly unstable. The family describes her as having been pretty, talented, and popular when she was young. She immigrated to Israel, and lived with her mother in a small apartment. There was tension between them. One day my mother ran away from home. The first person she met in the street was a taxi driver who took her to a hotel, one thing led to another, they had a relationship, and I was born.

I never met my father. I was raised by my grandmother. She also committed suicide. She overdosed on pills at home. This was the beginning of my rollercoaster ride from one foster family to another. My mother had not yet been hospitalized, but she felt she couldn't take responsibility for me. I assume she really couldn't take care of me. When I was four I was given to a foster family. This was very significant for me. Two years later my mother insisted on taking me back. Not long after, she was hospitalized. This is the first hospitalization episode I can remember. From time to time, between admissions to the hospital, she would visit me at my foster home. She gained weight from the drugs she was given, and that was difficult for me to see. I felt different and inferior to other children who had parents and siblings. When I lived in boarding school in Jerusalem she came to visit me once but as I had a family in Jerusalem I felt less isolated there.

I was "a street urchin" from a good home. Once, when I was back home again, she "threatened" to send me back to boarding school. For me this was good news.

I learned how to behave from watching how my friend's father told her to behave. I went back to live with my mother when she was in remission. This was not easy for me and at a certain point I had to hospitalize her. I was about seven or eight years old at the time.

Just before I started 5th grade she became more unstable. She felt it happening but tried to ignore it a little longer because she wanted to make me a birthday party. After my party when I was eleven she said she wanted to return to the hospital. Because she was so aware of her situation the doctors anticipated that she would only spend a short time in hospital. She was there for 18 months.

When I was twelve years old I was supposed to go home for Hanukkah vacation. Suddenly I was called to the principal's office. I instinctively knew this meant bad news. I thought – it is either grandpa or my mother. The principal said: "Your mother has passed away. I am sorry." I asked: "How?" and the reply was: "It appears that she committed suicide." I asked how and was told that she drowned herself. My first thought was that I should also commit suicide. I remember the principal saying "You know how much your mother loved you and was proud of you." I probably cried, I can't remember.

On the day of the funeral the social worker took me to the cemetery. I remember a white fabric, a shroud. When they lowered her the shroud creased, and I said, "She is being creased." I remember the Shiva as fun, because in the past when the family got together, everybody would fight with each other, and here for a whole week everything carried on peacefully; on the last day of the Shiva they began to fight again, and I was taken back to boarding school.

I came to the class and immediately told my friends what had happened. The children did not know how to react. The staff told me later that I was exploiting this tragedy, that I was wild, and that I turned it around so I would appear to be the victim... but I can't remember any of this.

My aunt also committed suicide. I once lived with her too. I think I don't know a single person who died a natural death. My grandfather is still alive but that doesn't mean that he will die of natural causes.

There was a time that I thought that when I reach the age of thirty six – the age that my mother was when she died – I will die. Kill myself. I was certain that this would happen to me. These thoughts were the thoughts of an adolescent who, like many adolescents, was experiencing a rollercoaster of strong emotions. I engaged in destructive behavior. It fascinated me.

After completing my army service I went abroad to visit my family. My cousin told me of more mental illness in the family, paranoia, depression, and lots of interesting characters... I am sure the problem is genetic, but apart from genetics, my grandparents should never have married. The combination of the two of them was problematic. The combination, and their relationship destroyed them and their children. I have the feeling that no one in my family is normal. What that says about me is a major dilemma for me.

All my life I actually knew where my father was, but I only ventured to see him when I was a student. I didn't really want to be in touch with him but wanted to meet him to see if there was mental illness on his side and in that way check out my potential. I found a normal family. This for me meant

I have normal genes from one side. Through my father I learned to appreciate my mother. She was competent, beautiful, and well educated. And she was sick.

Why did she commit suicide?

Why not? What did she have to live for? Mental illness is worse than any other disease... worse than being retarded. When she was sane she understood how insane she was when she had her attacks. She understood how pathetic she was. Because of her situation she knew she hurt the whole family. She felt that she was a burden, and she was smart enough to understand it. She understood how hard it was for me to grow up with a mother like that. Maybe she took her life in a moment of madness; perhaps she was not aware of what she was doing. But I think she knew. I am not angry, I understand what she did. She had no other choice.

Fears... I haven't yet discovered myself enough to say... Ok I have beaten this. I yearn to have a stable life. I am very rational and I pay the price. The demons may appear... but I want to prove that I am alright, especially to myself. Not especially only to myself. I believe that the genetics/ environmental impact is 50/50. I know there are theories for and against, but I believe that environment and society have a greater impact than genetics. I believe too that the people who influenced me did a good job. I am in control of my life, and the demons seem to be under control; but then again you never know.

I am not preoccupied with suicide. What I am concerned with is my success. And my measure of success is quite different from others'. I am preoccupied with my ability to establish a happy home. I do not believe that I'll kill myself... what I miss the most is a stable loving family of my own, something I never had. If I succeed in achieving this I'll feel that I have triumphed. I hope I'm on the right track.

Nothing was hidden in my life, and that was very good. My mother kept no secrets, at least not from me. I only lived with her for two or three years, but I feel that we spent our lives together. She never tried to trick me. For instance, my uncle didn't tell his wife everything about our family before they got married. He told her about my mother, but not about my aunt. Did he think that she wouldn't find out? Today they are divorced. You can't build a relationship without trust. I have had a boyfriend for couple of years now. My uncle told me not to tell him everything in the beginning. I was shocked. Was I supposed to hide this? Am I guilty of anything? I did the best I could under the circumstances, and I feel neither shame nor guilt. Perhaps this is the gift my mother bestowed upon me.

Why have you agreed to be interviewed?

The research question interested me and I'm interested in the outcomes; I thought that perhaps I could contribute in some way... I don't know what my contribution will be, but perhaps any piece of information might help in the future, and if I can contribute in any way, that makes me proud and happy.

SPOUSAL SUICIDE

In his book *"Survivors of Suicide"*, Albert Cain writes that his initial field of research was the act of suicide and its causes. His involvement in the area of suicide survivors evolved from his original research which was to identify and characterize signs which appeared before the suicide, and in this way assist in the prevention of future cases. In 1969, as part of his research, he interviewed widows and widowers, who were suicide survivors, and this led to a new field of research. Researchers found that the interviewees, whose spouses had committed suicide, suffered from lack of support in their grief and needed a place where they could share their difficulties, even many years after the suicide had occurred. The survivors shared many common problems, in particular the lack of legitimate expression of their feelings.

In many cases, spouses of people who have committed suicide suffer from shock and subsequent guilt for not having built a relationship which provided the support and assistance needed by their spouse, and ultimately for not being able to prevent the suicide. At the same time the surviving spouse feels rejected, angry, and guilty. In many cases the unresolved question concerning the reason for the suicide affects their ability to process their grief. My interviewees, whose spouse committed suicide, often talk about their closest friendship ending abruptly, and they feel that in retrospect society judges their relationship. Children who have lost a parent by suicide also question their parents' relationship. Marsha spoke about the loving relationship her parents had and quoted her mother as saying that her father always made her blush right up until his death.

In his book, Colin Pritchard[52] claims that the trauma of losing a spouse by suicide is second only to the trauma of parents losing a child by suicide. People whose spouses have committed suicide feel guilty for not recognizing

---

52 Pritchard, C. (1996). *Suicide - the Ultimate Rejection?*

the signs, thus not preventing the suicide. They also feel humiliated for apparently failing to build a relationship which was not strong enough to give their spouse the sense of security needed to share their distress. In many cases, spouses develop feelings of guilt and rejection, leading to the feeling that they had not been loved. Anger tends to deepen these feelings.

Losing a spouse is one of the most traumatic events experienced in a person's life time. Widowhood brings with it a multitude of difficulties such as raising the children alone, financial difficulties (which may increase when the primarily bread winner dies), but the most intense emotion experienced is the feeling of loneliness. When suicide is the cause of widowhood, these difficulties are exacerbated. Marriage is considered a contract, and when one partner commits suicide they unilaterally and unpredictably choose to break the contract with the person who was to be a lifelong partner. In addition to the question of the reason for the suicide, the question so often asked is "…how could my spouse leave me like this?" The surviving spouse feels as if a part of them has been severed. Even when the relationship was a good one, friends begin to question whether things were really as good as they appeared. My interviewees talked about subtle hints from their friends indicating that there may have been something in their own (the surviving spouse's) behavior that might have contributed to, or caused the suicide. As Hannah said, when she met other men after her husband's suicide, she wouldn't talk about it, so they wouldn't think she "had done something to him…"

In addition to their own grief, the surviving spouse (who is at the same time a parent), has to cope with their children's grief and difficulties in understanding the situation. Some of the dilemmas they face are whether they should tell their children that it was a suicide? When? To all their children? At what age? These are some of the questions I was asked when participating in a professional capacity, in support groups for surviving spouses. In his book *Children of Suicide: the Telling and the Knowing* when he published findings from another study, Albert Cain[53] said that the question of *when* to tell, must address both the difficulties of the surviving parent, and at the same time the difficulties of the children. The time that passes between the suicide and speaking of it to the children is also significant. Cain claims that the approach of 'tell everything regardless of the consequences' is not necessarily the best approach. Each family's situation is unique, and an appropriate approach is needed. He writes of parents who tried to speak to their children, but ran into a wall of resistance. Then there were other parents who talked about delaying

53   Cain, A.C. (2002), *Children of Suicide: the Telling and the Knowing.* Omega (65)2, 124-136

the discussion as a way of buying time, feeling that the more time that lapsed from the suicide itself, the better the surviving parent could control their feelings and anger, and hence they could provide the best form of comfort for their children. They felt that this would make it easier for the surviving parent to speak to the children in a way that would facilitate the children's assimilation, understanding, and processing of the information provided. One interviewee claimed that, had he told his children about their mother's suicide right after it happened, they would have hated her, or him, or both.

One of the findings pertaining to the question of when parents should tell their children has revealed that the age of the surviving child at the time of the suicide is an important factor. In general, parents try to spare young children from knowing all the details, but, as I know from my own story and from what I have discovered from the people I interviewed, children do know, even if they have not been told the whole story. Cain talks about a seven year old girl who told her therapist that her father killed himself, and immediately added "... but don't tell my mother, she thinks it was a car accident."

The main message for the surviving parent should therefore be that even if the suicide is not discussed on a regular basis, children should be encouraged and should feel free to talk and ask about it whenever they feel like.

Joel

When I arrive at Joel's moshav (an agricultural village), he's still busy with the administration of the morning milking of the cows, so I join him. We sit in his immaculate office adjoining the dairy. He's working on a sophisticated computer program, which analyzes the quality of the milk and health of each cow, in order to achieve the optimum results he matches the best cows with the best bulls. "I wish that I could find myself a match this easily" he jokes.

I'll tell you about Orit. Two years before she committed suicide she said that she didn't feel well. Apparently she realized that it was an emotional disorder. She was hospitalized, given medication, and we were under the impression that everything was under control. She saw a psychiatrist for a year and a half and he prescribed appropriate medication for her. After a year and a half she disappeared from home. We searched for her for four days. After four days they came at night to tell me that she had killed herself and had done it in a very brutal manner. The police were really very understanding. The children were aged 11 and 13 at the time.

In hindsight we realized that she had ceased taking her medication. But even before that I had the feeling that she wasn't cooperating in therapy. She blamed the doctors, me... and our relationship. The situation was complicated. Two months before her suicide, the doctors told her that she wasn't cooperating, that she was blaming everyone and everything around her, and she wasn't doing anything to help herself. Obviously I wasn't the only one who felt this way. But the doctors refused to hospitalize her and she deteriorated. Her depression got worse and deepened. But she never talked about suicide, never mentioned the word, not verbally and not in writing. She didn't leave a note. I have only one thing to say, she left me with a "glowing light" in my life, even though I still can't see the light at the end of the tunnel. I have no doubt that she was extremely intelligent, and this affected her decision. She couldn't come to terms with her condition. I remember now that in the last months of her life, she often called many of her girlfriends, and they cut the conversation short as they just couldn't listen to her anymore.

What bothers me to this day is that on the day she disappeared I was in an important meeting. She called looking for me and I didn't know. This bothers me to no end. I wish I knew what she wanted to tell me, even though I know she would have done it just the same. In her bag there was a list of things she planned to take with her, petrol, a jerry can...and she drove to the Carmel Mountains, to the area where we often used to go on weekends. She poured petrol all over the car and lit it. The car actually didn't catch on fire, but she suffocated to death. I met the person who found her and spoke to him. It was important for me to meet him at the place where it happened.

Life wasn't easy for her. I wasn't the most flexible of husbands, and she was complicated, but we had a very interesting life together. I really admired her. We travelled extensively both in Israel and abroad. We did lots of things together and we had many mutual interests. We both loved nature, animals, plants, geology, history...and she loved living here in our little village. Our lives were not easy, but it's difficult for me to gauge whether this affected her decision, if at all.

Life with her wasn't easy. For instance, on the Saturday of our son's bar mitzvah, she refused to go to the synagogue. This was a difficult situation. She had lots of problems in her life, and she couldn't really cope with them. This is what I think, but no one really knows.

She found out that she had cancer, and she just didn't cope at all with the sickness together with her emotional problems. I tried to give her as much support as I could. I really loved her just as she was.

Do I fill the void for my children, do I fill their world? I don't know. One of my daughters is really open with me and we talk about everything. But it's not easy for me. Just think of it... she has to go with her father to buy a bra. although sometimes her girlfriends' mothers, who really like her, help her.

Are you angry with Orit?

The kids are really angry, and ashamed of what she did. They don't like to engage in any discussion surrounding her death. Am I angry? I can't say. As time passes I miss her more and more. I meet many women, I am looking for someone for myself, and when I meet someone it only magnifies the difference between them and her. I try not to compare.

Actually, now I have many more friends. I don't know how things would have been had she still been alive. I travel quite a bit and I have made many different friends. People are not suspicious of me...people, society, are kind and understanding to a widower. And women friends are always trying to introduce me to new women.

Our household runs on mutual respect and help; we cook together, one washes the dishes, the other folds the laundry, everyone pitches in, however the greatest burden of responsibility of course is on my shoulders. Also, as we are a farming family we spend a great deal of time at home. Already in the first week, the children said "We are all carrying on as usual, and we will still go on all our weekend trips." They asked me to be in the house every morning, so at 6:30 every morning I'm up and ready for them. Also at lunchtime when they come home from school there's always a meal ready and waiting for them. All this has been very important to them.

The community where we live in our moshav is very concerned, very caring, loving and warm. After it happened, friends attended to all the bureaucracy involved, and at the school, everyone was tremendously helpful. During the "shiva" , hundreds of people came to our home and the support was overwhelming and important to me. Our extended family also lives close by.

I always say that men cry at night. I didn't cry at the funeral. We do have commemorative services. At the commemoration that we held two years after she died, friends of mine asked if they could participate. They wanted to be with me and share my pain. The children still can't bring themselves to read anything at the commemoration services.

When we go on our outings, it's really hard for me if we go anywhere in the vicinity of places we went to together. And if I start to talk about her my kids ask me to stop. They say it's enough. They completely close up and all conversation ceases.

Sometimes I have the feeling that Orit is kind of saying "here, you're left with the problems and the pain", and that this is how she is punishing me. So yes, I guess in fact, I am angry! After all, we spent 17 years together, we had both good and difficult times, and divorce was not what separated us.

Nancy

Nancy is Adam's mother. Adam's story appears at the beginning of this book. When I submitted my thesis proposal, which its topic was "The impact of parental suicide on the child," Nancy, who worked at the university, saw my proposal, and reading the title she broke down in tears. "My husband committed suicide", she told me. "You interview people whose parents have committed suicide, perhaps you can convince my son to talk to you". A few years later, after I had completed my thesis, and a long time after I interviewed Adam, who in the meantime got married, Nancy and I met in a cafe in Jerusalem.

Al was a wonderful father and husband. Our marriage was a romantic one. We would kiss and hug. We were always open about any problems and were always involved in our boys' lives. My husband was always involved in everything the kids did and was a real personality in our village. All the parties took place in our home. Al would pick up all the kids in the neighborhood. He was always surrounded by an entourage of kids. We loved to hike and take trips, and the kids slept out in tents from the age of three months. Our family life was great. Our lives were so enmeshed... when he couldn't sleep, I couldn't sleep, when he didn't eat, neither did I, and when we ran into financial difficulties, I went to the bank to take out a loan. When he died, his friends told me they would pay back the loan, but I didn't let them pay back a cent. In a relationship such as ours, the blow of his death was even greater. Al was a fighter and if he were to die, he should have died in the war. He saved our neighbor from suicide, twice... He was a contractor and had his own business; he left me some unfinished projects and debts -taxes, social security, and the banks. All this fell on my shoulders. People kept asking me whether there were any signs hinting at what he did. It was so out of character that I had no idea, but in retrospect, when I began to dig, I remembered two very significant events. When times got tough he used to say "my future is behind me"; and from the time we owned our home there were occasions when I suggested that we sell the house but he never wanted to. In the last week of his life, before he died, he said, "Nancy, I'm ready to sell the house" and I said it would be a new beginning. When I look back on my life with Al, there is just one black cloud that still hangs over me. I used to attend a weekly night out with my social group and I used to say that this was 'my time'. If you want to do something with me, don't make it on this night. A few months later, exactly during 'my time', he and his partner arranged an event. I told him I wasn't coming and this was the biggest fight we ever had. And I remember one more issue. From the age of four, until I was eighteen, I was a dancer. Over the first few years that we were married, I told Al that I wanted to study dance seriously. But because of our financial circumstances, he said we couldn't afford it and he wouldn't allow me to pursue it. I feel that I haven't been able to overcome my resentment to this day.

However, many of our friends were envious of our loving relationship. The most difficult thing was that I was left a widow with three children, aged 12.5, eight and seven. Immediately after it happened my brother paid all our debts without any help from Al's family. After that there were more debts that we had to pay and Al's family said that they wouldn't give me a cent, that it was my problem to solve alone. While Al was alive his family always lent him money for the business, but after he died, they evicted me from our home because the house was in his name, not mine.

For four or five years I asked them to help me as I had no means to repay the debts. Gradually I managed to repay all the debts to the banks, taxation department, etc., right to the last penny. Al's family tried to turn the children against me and my family. Al's brother never liked me and had always been against our marriage. He even accused me of being responsible for Al's death. In a way I can understand his family. Their son is dead and I'm alive.

I should mention that on the morning of his suicide I realized something was wrong when Al hadn't called me by 10:00AM as he used to four or five times a day. I knew that he was supposed to be at a friend's house and I called just to be told that Al left in a very bad mood. Later that day, 16 years ago, which was the eve of a holiday of lighting bonfires and celebrating so all our friends were out celebrating. My closest friends organized a search party and called the police. In the middle of the night, the local chief of police received a message that a burnt out car was found. He told them to look for a body near the car. It seems that Al took all the files from the office, burnt them and then shot himself. His friends identified the body and at 10:00AM the next morning the police notified me. I decided that the funeral would be that same night. I didn't want to wait. I was exhausted and couldn't face another sleepless night.

The funeral took place at 10PM with thousands of people attending. They came from all over the country, from near and far. The funeral took place after dark, which gave it a special feeling. Al and the rabbi had always worked toward tolerance and understanding between the religious and secular sections of society and when the rabbi delivered his eulogy, there wasn't a dry eye in the crowd. The Shiva (seven mourning days) was constantly overflowed with people who came to express their sympathy. Our friends saw to food, cleaning the house, shopping, cooking and took care of everything.

The children: Abe didn't say a word. Tom cried a little which was so very hard for me to watch, and Adam was mad at the whole world and blamed me for everything. He said to me: you married him, gave birth to me, and everything is your fault.

Al left a suicide note of three lines: "I love you; guard our most precious - Adam, Tom and Abe; and don't betray me!"

Everyone heard about his last request and gossip raged... I didn't know where to hide. What to do with that sentence.

During the first year after he died, I left my job and went to work at the university. I thought that I'd give it a year for things to settle. Almost every day I received a phone call from one or another of the boys' teachers. The most painful thing was that all our friends, or supposed to be friends, who had enjoyed themselves with us, and who we had entertained in our home over the past 20 years, abandoned me. I can honestly say that I was left with three close friends. After about six months I went to visit a friend whom I used to help out a lot. When I asked her why she hadn't come to see me she replied that she wasn't prepared to get involved with my problems.

As I said, during the Shiva all our old friends came. They cried and I even had to console them. But at the end of the week, I decided that I had to get back to a normal routine, and I should do it quickly. My father told me that he would stand by me and would support me whatever I decided to do. This really helped me to carry on. I decided to leave the apartment and move somewhere else. Over the years, my mother always came on vacations with us and the kids wouldn't agree to go without her. Two years after Al died, she became ill and couldn't come with us, but she said that she would pay for us to go on vacation and told the children she would come with us again next year. We left for our vacation, but returned immediately in time to take my mother to the hospital. Three weeks later she died. So we lost my mother and Al within two and half years.

Adam refused to stay home alone. If I returned home late from work, he had the whole neighborhood and the police out looking for me. He also wouldn't allow me to date anyone. He tried to become the man of the house and there was a constant war between us. Because of my guilt feelings and the pressure on me, it was hard for me to cope with him. I decided to get him to therapy. Adam kicked the therapist in the knee and that was the end of therapy with the first one. He broke the window in the office of the second one... and to the third he said "don't get involved in things that are none of your business". Then I decided that I would tell each of the kids, according to their level of understanding, what had really happened. I had never talked to them about it before. At one point things with Adam were so difficult that I wanted him to leave home. Adam said to me "Do you want to throw me out?" and the school counselor said the same thing. Another therapist said to me that I was responsible for my children's behavior.

Adam asked a lot of questions. He wouldn't accept what I told him. The other two listened when I told them, but did not react in any way. When I told the kids, each one processed what I had told them as best they could, according to their level of understanding. The boys attended different schools. Adam has been just another 'number' in his school. His grades were so low at times that they told him that if he didn't improve he wouldn't be able to go on to high school. I also told him that if I was called to school one more time I would take him out of school and send him to boarding school... and he would have to pay for his studies. It was only when he was in his last year of high school, that he started to open up. He had to write an essay for his matriculation exams and he decided to write about what he had been through. His grade for that essay was 97%.

Over the years I gave my kids lots of love. I didn't have money, but I sacrificed my life for six or seven years and our relationship thrived. My sons would talk to me about their girlfriends and about everything else. Six or seven years after I finished paying off all my debts I bought an apartment. When I applied for my job at the university, they held a meeting to decide whether to hire a widow with three children... ultimately I got the job and after that I could see the light at the end of the tunnel. However, when I asked my boss for some time off to go and buy an apartment he said he would give me 'one day'. At 4:30PM I found an apartment and when I excitedly told him he said "What are you so happy about... your husband is six feet under!"

Today, at work, I am flourishing... my co-workers really like me. I was even voted 'outstanding employee'. I am the head of an outstanding department, I supervise many students and I feel like their grandmother. We are all very close. I have also started to date. This is a good stage in my life, but I haven't formed any serious relationships yet.

I understood that I needed therapy. Social security provides therapy for widows and widowers. The first time I went I decided to watch from the sidelines. When I started to talk, I said that my husband was killed in an accident. After three months I gradually began to come out of my shell and decided to tell the truth. The group sat in stunned silence till I finished. When these free meetings ended, I decided to continue with therapy and found a counselor whom I liked. These were difficult times but during that period I grew and got stronger.

Three days before the yearly memorial service I went to a concert. I sang and danced. Then three days later I sobbed. I told myself that I found balance. I could both laugh and cry.

When Adam joined the army, he said goodbye to his brothers, but said nothing to me. He started to walk away, but then he realized that he was leaving home and he ran back and gave me such a huge hug... When my boys enlisted to the army I was left alone. One of them was in Lebanon for three years, the other was involved in a civil uprising during his army service. I don't have to tell you that I didn't sleep nights during their army service. I never stood in their way and allowed them to enlist in whichever unit they wanted to. When my youngest received an award for being an outstanding soldier, I brought cookies for the whole unit. I said to myself, wow, their father was a paratrooper, he should have been here for this, but I was there by myself.

After their army service, Adam decided to go to the United States on a coast to coast trip. Later, when he decided to get married it was a difficult time. He didn't want me to walk him down the aisle, he told me he preferred me to wait under the marriage canopy with the young couple walking towards me. I asked him if he wanted to go to the cemetery; he said no. Four days before the wedding I went to the cemetery, to Al, and the rest of the deceased members of our family.

About a year ago, Tom told me he was going to do a workshop on interpersonal relationships. When it was over I was told that the only one who spoke positively about their mother was my son. After he had done it, I decided that I also wanted to attend such a workshop. The workshop was great and helped me open up. It gave me confidence, it calmed me, and I felt that nothing could throw me off balance (except my kids). I came to the conclusion that I was a good person, a person of merit, and that I am able to stand on my own two feet, unlike in the past when I felt worthless, especially without a man.

I started to wear bright colors and people who hadn't seen me for a long time, said "it's not just the clothes but it's the twinkle in your eyes". I think today I am open and honest; my three sons are now supportive of me and forming new relationships. I have learnt that the friends I have today are those I have chosen. There is nothing more important than my family and I am at peace with myself. Having a man in my life is not a major issue, if I don't have one I'll be fine, and if one comes along, he'll be a lucky man. I like the Nancy of today. I look in the mirror and I see a happy woman, life is good. I think I have matured since Al's suicide. With four men in the house I was the princess, yet I look better now than I did twenty years ago. I love my life, work out, walk, and have enrolled in a mediation course. I think I can pat myself on the back. I have raised three wonderful boys. I am proud of them. I have reached this stage because sixteen years after Al's death, at the memorial service attended by family and friends I decided to speak out. "Your father left a legacy that I should take care of the most precious things in our life, you boys. I happily dedicate my life to you. I raised you to be wonderful human beings and although I was alone, I accompanied you to your barmitzvahs, the army, and to your wedding, Adam. Each of you chose your own path and I never stood in your way. I was happy even though I was alone." After I spoke, my three boys broke down in tears. Tom has forgiven his father even though it's still hard for him. Adam wants to learn more about his father. And I, who have risen from the bottom of the pit, have managed to emerge whole, and at peace with myself. I have three wonderful children, close friends and family who love me, and I love them. I chose life and I am living it to the full. I enjoy the little things in life, the sunrise, the sunset, and the twitter of the birds as I walk. Life is good.

You barely mentioned this hard sentence from his suicide note, "don't betray me".

This sentence was so hard for me. I didn't know how to interpret it. At first it was as if he was telling me not to go out, to stay alone. But on second thoughts perhaps he meant, don't betray our way of life, our beliefs, the values we wanted for our children, and the love of the land. The fact that this sentence in his note became public knowledge and gave rise to many rumors, bothered me. But it stopped bothering me after a few years. I know one thing, I was told that when Al was deep in debt, he said "Do anything you want to me, but don't touch Nancy".

I went through every stage of mourning, I knew exactly when there was closure and I remember saying to myself, "I will walk with my head held high and no one can say a thing about me that will hurt me".

What hurts me is that Al missed the boys' barmitzvahs, their induction into the army, weddings and grandchildren. This pain never leaves me, and he doesn't know what he missed. It's more painful because he was such a wonderful father. He would close the business at four o'clock and regardless of what was left to do he would come home to be with the family.

How can a person choose to leave something so wonderful and do what he did?! He must have been temporarily insane.

Why did he do it? His parents were involved in his financial difficulties, and when the police came because of the debts, he simply broke down. Even though I had my difficulties with his parents, I always told the children to visit them whenever they could. I think the worst thing that can happen to a parent is to bury their child, so I really do pity them.

I don't envy anyone with property or money, since Al's suicide was because of financial problems. I told myself that money would never be a governing factor in my life. When I look back on these past years, I don't know how I got through them. My closest friends told me that they don't know if they could have survived what I went through. I am proud of myself for the path I have taken. My success makes me stand up straight and due to this I feel I have grown the five cm that were always missing. No one will make me bitter; life is good, I am happy that my kids know that I am always there for them; and this is the most important thing for me.

BEREAVED PARENTS

The American psychologist Iris Bolton in her book *My Son, My Son,*[54] written after her son's suicide, shares her experience and suggests ways to assist other families to cope with a child's suicide. She claims that what helped her cope was her ability to talk about the experience openly with the other family members, but felt that real progress was made only when she accepted that the burden of guilt lay in part with her son, accepting that there were aspects of his personality and behavior, not only the behavior of the people around him, that contributed to his decision to commit suicide. Another difficulty she was confronted with was the feeling that people were pointing a finger at her, but she coped with this too when she understood that this was their way of coping with their own feelings of guilt, pain, and grief.

She also talks about the depression she suffered following her son's suicide. Depression is a reaction which is both expected, yet at the same time threatening. She says that dealing with the depression became easier when she accepted that it would take time, and in fact she began to view it as a 'gift' because it brought her closer to understanding the depths of depression to which her son had sunk. Bolton, however, had the ability and the strength to get out from under, the strength that her son lacked. Advice she gives to surviving parents is to be aware of their child's pain; when the child appears to experience more pain or anguish than the 'normal' difficulties experienced at that age, parents must be strong enough to admit that there is a problem, and seek professional assistance (even if the child rejects intervention). After experiencing a suicide, the family, too, needs professional help, and it is important that the survivors see this help as legitimate.

After the suicide of one's child, parents are only able to heal and move on once they are able to accept the fact that the question as to why he did it will never really be fully answered. However parents must understand and

---

54   Bolton, I. (1983). *My Son, My son: A guide to healing after death, loss or Suicide.* Atlanta: Balton press.

accept that it was the child's responsibility. In the case of a child's suicide, parents tend to blame themselves and often connect it to a single event, such as a reaction by the parents to something the child said or did. Bolton claims that the decision to commit suicide is the outcome of a sequence of events, and a parental act or omission may, at the most, be the trigger to a decision the child had already made. One of the most valuable tools she sees as crucial to the parents' rehabilitation is a support system, including support groups or self-help groups, where people who have experienced the same tragedy and struggled with the same difficulties can help others cope.

A recent study which examined work conducted on parental grief between the years 1975-2013, found that self-blame, guilt, and shame are common amongst bereaved parents, and these feelings often lead to post-traumatic reactions and depression; nevertheless researchers note that the issue got little attention in works on bereavement and grief.[55] Losing a child is considered to be the most severe loss in a parent's lifetime, and recovery is complex, lengthy, and never complete. However, losing a child through suicide is immeasurably more difficult.

One of the best ways for suicide survivors to cope with the suicide and its impact is to join a support group, as here the parents are able to share this massive burden with people who have experienced the same loss. Here they can share common feelings and coping methods with others. In such a group a feeling of community and belonging evolves, and this in itself provides support to its members. The support group helps its members reject the stigma. Parents whose children have committed suicide face blame from society for their child's death, so for them the group is a unique place to meet other people to whom this happened, who are going through the same horrible experience, and here finally they can feel that they are 'not alone in their suffering' as many of my interviewees put it. For parents this is the only place they may feel protected from the unbearable blame, the blame of the death of one's own child. Cain and La Ferriere[56] also stressed the importance of peer intervention and support for the bereaved.

It is not only that parents feel that society blames them. They themselves are engaged in an endless process of self-torture, attempting to reconstruct events, actions, things they did or said to their children that

---

55 Duncan, C. and Cacciatore, J. (2015). A systematic review of the peer-reviewed literature on self-blame, guilt and shame. Omega 71(4)

56 Cain, A.C. and La Freniere, L. (2015). Peer interaction of parentally bereaved children and adolescents: a qualitative study. Omega: Journal of Death and Dying 72(2)

might have caused this terrible act. After the death of a child, any insulting statement, any demonstration of anger, even the slightest one, takes on disproportionate significance. Naomi, for example, recalls that she refused her son's request to buy him a subscription to a youth newspaper. "But this shouldn't cause a suicide, should it?" she asked me.

Tracy

Seven years prior to this interview Tracy and Ariel's son committed suicide, leaving a wife and a two years old son.

This coming Friday is the memorial service. It has been seven years. He was our middle son. He had a brother and sister. He was a very stubborn child, a quality I now see reflected in his son. For instance when he got angry at his high school he announced that he would not go to the graduation ceremony... and he didn't go! But he did go to the office later to collect his report card. When he was a kid, I couldn't find any way of punishing him that had any effect on him. If I told him he couldn't leave the house, he retorted that he didn't want to go out any way and this always took the wind out of my sails. Once he made up his mind that was it. After 6th grade I had to take him out of school because the teacher asked the students to copy questions and answers from the board and he refused to do it. Every couple of days I was called to the school for a meeting with his teachers.

From the time he went into the army, at the age of eighteen, he never came back to live at home. He served in a combined agricultural and military unit in the army and immediately upon leaving the army went to live on a kibbutz. He studied, and then got married, so I don't really know what affected him, what triggered it. I do remember that on one occasion he did come back home from the army very depressed. He had been in Lebanon where he witnessed our forces accidentally firing on our own forces, and he was right there. But I can't say for sure whether this is connected to his suicide. I only found out about this incident when we were sitting 'Shiva'. There was also one time when he came home to Jerusalem, from Beirut, and he was depressed and refused to eat. Another idea that arose was the fact that my husband was a child during the Holocaust and this may have had an effect on my son, but who knows?

If there were any particular events in my son's life that affected his behavior, I cannot put my finger on them because as I said, he didn't live at home from about the age of eighteen, and how much can you gauge from visits?

He got married and we didn't even know he was depressed or that he was in therapy. He was about to complete his Master's degree. One Saturday morning we received a call that he was taken to intensive care because he had attempted suicide. This was seven months before he actually committed suicide. He was hospitalized in a psychiatric ward for a month. I visited him two to three times a day, and I didn't even know *how* to talk to him, what I was *allowed* to talk to him about, whether to ask him about "the act"... and I didn't tell anyone. I just said that he was in hospital, but I didn't tell them what had happened and why he was there. It took a while before I even told my only sister. To this day, I can't tell most people about it. I'm sure you understand my situation. I am still very angry with myself, because by not talking about either the suicide or my son, I too am contributing to the creation of the "taboo" surrounding suicide, but I can't help myself. I still tell people that "he was sick", and leave it to people to interpret this any way they like. There are some people who I feel won't be judgmental and I can talk to them and tell them right away. But there are others whose reactions I'm not sure about and I don't feel able to tell them outright that he committed suicide.

In the psychiatric ward no one really took any notice of us, the parents. Not a word was spoken to us. I told the psychologist that I wanted to hear about, and try to understand, what had happened to our son. She just said, "He did a terrible thing." That was horrible for me since I didn't know whether, if I spoke to him, it would make things worse for him or not. In theory I knew something about suicide, but when you are personally involved, theory doesn't help. In a way his suicide attempt was more traumatic for me than his death ... can you believe it?

He had plans to enter a professional retraining program, and he expressed doubts about whether he would be successful. I began to feel that he was changing in some ways but I couldn't really put my finger on it. In hindsight I don't even know if I could have helped him. I saw him two days before he committed suicide and I didn't really see any signs.

"Bang"... that's suicide ... and it's my son!

When you told me about your father, it really affected me. My daughter-in-law told their son what had happened; he was kindergarten age and she told him that his father had committed suicide. She said to him, "We don't talk to other people about it, but you can talk about it to your grandparents." One day I came to pick him up from kindergarten and one of the little girls asked innocently, "Where is your father?" He didn't answer. I tensed up immediately.

His reactions always interest me, and I do talk about his father to him in all kinds of different situations. One day we were walking past the school that my son attended, and I said to my grandson, "This is the primary school that your father attended." Then out of the blue he said to me "Actually if my father came to life now, he would be a skeleton, but I would have a father." Comments like this show you why I'm interested in children's reactions. When I went with my grandson to the playground he always latched onto father figures, and of course I couldn't and wouldn't explain to these men why he did this.

Obviously a situation such as ours affects the entire family. My daughter had to fill out a questionnaire for a job, and on it they asked if anyone in the family had committed suicide. I don't really understand why they asked this, and why it was relevant. She didn't know whether to answer honestly or to hide it.

At the memorial service we had for him we told people that we were recording the things they had to say. My other son didn't say a word. I asked him why. "Don't you have a single thing to say about your brother?" He replied, "I just can't!" Even three years later he still couldn't talk about it.

If I had the chance to meet other parents after their child was hospitalized following a suicide attempt, I feel that perhaps I could help them, but I don't know how to reach out and find them. I think that had I met a parent who had experienced a suicide in the family *then* (when my son was hospitalized), the meeting could have helped me. When we were sitting 'Shiva', a friend whose niece had committed suicide, visited me. She suggested that I meet with the mother. When I called the girl's mother she said to me, "But my daughter didn't commit suicide, she just took pills!" to which I replied, "My son also *just* took pills"...

My husband also harbored a lot of anger, but he kept it all inside. It was anger mixed with some understanding. Actually we couldn't really understand the depths of despair to which our son sank. Our friends still can't understand the fact that just as there is cancer which eats away at the body, there is also cancer which eats away at the soul. Society's message is so strong, that whether you accept it or not, it eats into our consciousness. I feel as if they are asking us, "What sort of parents are you?"...the blame is automatically cast onto the parents. This is the case even in psychiatry text books.

We talk a lot about our son. We don't talk about *what* happened, that's true, but he's with us. The thing that is the most difficult is that under these circumstances, time does not heal.

Naomi

It happened to us on October 6th, seven years ago. Our son left the house and simply said "I'm going out for a drive"... and he never came back. He was a kid who always came home on time, and he was supposed to be at the army recruiting center, the next morning. We knew that he had to get up early. For a couple of weeks before he left that day he had been quite upset about what was happening regarding his recruitment. He was unhappy with the unit the army had assigned him to. He was rather inclined to spend time alone reading books, listening to music, and sometimes playing chess or basketball with friends. He didn't go to parties or discos. He was tall, thin, quiet, and very intelligent with a great sense of humor. He loved math and physics, and learning in general. Daniel was eighteen years and two months old.

That same evening, just before leaving the house, he gave me a book saying, "read this and give it to dad to read, too", and then he left. I even said to him "be careful", referring of course to the driving. I read the book he left me thinking that I'd speak to him about it in the morning, and then I went to sleep. After about an hour and a half I woke up with an anxious, nervous feeling, not typical of me at all, and I got up. I saw that he wasn't in his room, nor was he in his brother's room. His brother was in the army at the time. Then on his brother's bed I noticed that there was an antique gun that he had been given for his Bar Mitzvah. I became more anxious wondering what that gun was doing there. I woke my husband and told him that Daniel was not home yet. He suggested that we wait a little longer but I asked him to check if *his* gun was in its place. His gun was gone. He, too, started to worry. We called the police, his friends, and a search went out for him. One of my friends came over to our house to sit and wait with me.

My husband and daughter joined the search parties, together with the police and some other friends. At 5 o'clock in the morning, I took off all my jewellery and said to my friend, "I think that he's not coming home anymore." At 5:30 AM, my husband and daughter returned. They said that he had been found, and the police reported that he had committed suicide.

At that very moment, my world collapsed. Up to that point I had felt that my world was intact, but now it was all over; it was not the same world. The only sentence I could utter over and over again was: "My life is over!" Friends who came over to offer their condolences said to me that my life was not over, that there would be good times ahead, grandchildren, etc. but

I couldn't see that... essentially my life was over. Physically I felt that an axe had smashed down on my right shoulder, and a third of the right side of my body from top to bottom was paralyzed. I had to tell myself that I wasn't paralyzed. I finally realized that the feeling that a third of me was paralyzed was because one of three of my children had been torn from me, so it was no surprise that my right side felt paralyzed. He was our youngest child, and he was my right hand around the house.

Every morning I thought I'd stop breathing, and every night I was sure that I would not survive until morning. In fact, sometimes when I recall the first week, I don't understand how I did survive. Honestly! It wasn't a conscious decision to go on for my other children, I just survived. Many different memories come back and flood my mind. My daughter said to me immediately after the event, "I hope you don't go and do something crazy with dad's gun" to which I simply replied, "No, I have two more children, a husband, and I have to care for my family." I told my son, who came home from the army, "He was your little brother, you loved him, and you're allowed to mourn." I talked, but I don't know where the words came from. For a few weeks I had no appetite, I couldn't put a morsel into my mouth. I lost so much weight that I was able to fit into Daniel's jeans. I wore them for a few months.

For the first month I didn't go back to work. My friends took turns to come and sit with me and take me for walks around our neighborhood. And the whole time I just cried. I couldn't sleep at night. I had two jobs and after a month both my bosses came and asked me to come back to work. To get to one of my workplaces I had to take the bus that Daniel used to take to school. At first I simply couldn't get onto the bus. I used to take two and three other buses, just so I wouldn't have to go on that bus. Later on one of my friends came and rode on the bus with me; this made it easier for me. My girlfriends simply saved me. Some of our friends were absolutely amazing, they remained in touch, came to the memorial services, were willing to talk to us about it, but others distanced themselves from us.

I met Debbie. She was in a support group for parents who had a child commit suicide and we started to attend the meetings together. The group met once every three weeks. This really saved me. The leader of the group was supportive, clever, and had a heart of gold. Within the group people formed strong bonds and we stayed in touch even outside the group meetings.

During that time I survived from one meeting until the next. What really helped me was that at the meetings I could talk to people just like myself, and I could see that they weren't monsters, they weren't bad people. Amongst the many feelings that washed over me after it happened was the feeling that I must be a really bad person. Paradoxically, every new story that I heard in the group was even more devastating than my own. Sometimes there were stories of prolonged mental illness or drugs. After hearing these stories I was sometimes filled with hope that my son might come back because life had not been so difficult for him and in fact he didn't really have a good reason to commit suicide, so maybe it didn't really happen! Maybe it was a mistake! For a long time I had a feeling that he might still come home. This feeling often helped me fall asleep at night.

For nine months I didn't go near my husband. After nine months it felt like some sort of reverse pregnancy; I stopped crying every day. At first we went to therapy. This was terrible for me. Our therapist was totally out of touch with where I was in my grief and I related to this therapy as if it was another punishment that I deserved.

We lost touch with Daniel's friends and their parents, apart from meeting them at his memorial services. The mother of one of his friends said to me, "Everyone was shocked and frightened, and felt that if this happened to you, it could happen to any of us." Before the last memorial service, three of his friends called us and asked if they could come over and visit... just like that, out of the blue. On the one hand it was really difficult; on the other hand it was good.

The night of the... the suicide, it's still hard for me to say that word, actually on the night before, I felt like I was on the verge of a big breakthrough at work. Suddenly everything I was teaching fell into place, and I had found the solution to a number of problems. This happened exactly that day. The irony of the situation was that the courses I taught had to do with improving the mental health of students in the classroom, encouraging communication between the students, developing self-awareness, and the acquisition of tools to deal with real life. That is what I was teaching when the tragedy struck. I felt that fate was laughing in my face. It's like when the shoemaker's children go barefoot, but worse than that. Here I was, 'the expert'... it was as if someone had thrown a bucket of tar in my face!

I announced that I would no longer be teaching these courses. This announcement was received with understanding. Instead of teaching I was put in charge of computer data, since I didn't want to go back to working with kids. I put in a request to set up a library for teachers at the school, and later on I gradually went back to teaching, but just a little. At both my jobs, the supervisors, management, and colleagues, were very understanding and considerate.

Did he leave a note or anything written at all?

He highlighted two lines in the book he gave me to read. It is actually the diary of a soldier who was killed in the Lebanon war. It's a book that Daniel's siblings loved, and they gave it to him to read before he went into the army. At a certain point, the boy who wrote the book hinted at suicide. He volunteered to go on a dangerous mission during the war even though he was not a combat soldier. He was killed there. There were a number of similarities between that soldier and my son. They were both good at math, they were both tall and thin, they both liked Russian literature, Kafka, etc. The two lines which my son highlighted were: "I believe that the *interesting things* in life are unattainable, apart from in our dreams." And Daniel, in place of the words 'interesting things' wrote in pencil the word 'happiness', and so the sentence changed to: 'I believe that *happiness* in life is unattainable, except in our dreams'.

The second sentence that Daniel highlighted was: 'It's not external factors that hold you back, it's you, that holds yourself back'.

In fact a few weeks earlier, Daniel had shown me a short story in the book that the same soldier had written when he was in 8th grade. If I have any regrets, it's because in the courses I taught, there is a topic about recognizing the poignant messages in written texts, and I just missed this one. The short story was about a youth who walks along a straight road, with no bends or curves. The youth constantly wants to leave the road, but he continues on. He continues expressionless and not hesitating, perhaps thinking that 'it won't happen to me'. In the middle of the road he suddenly drops and doesn't get up. His body is discovered in the morning. The road was a dead end; a small sign clearly stated this at the beginning of the road. I didn't relate at all to the details that they found his body, and that the road was a dead-end. Here he talked about the meaning of life; but I was only concerned with the fact that the boy wrote the story when he was in 8th grade. The other thing I thought about, but said nothing because I didn't want to project my logic on him, was that the idea of a dead-end road refers to vehicles and not to people, since there is no dead-end for people, there is always another option, you can always turn around and go back or find another way...but I didn't tell him this. Maybe he was trying to tell me something through this story and perhaps I simply didn't understand, and I didn't relate to it at all?

In the first year after his death lots of memories came flooding back to me, and I dreamt a lot. When he was little and as he was growing up I used to write detail of things he said and did. Suddenly many of the things that I had written took on new meaning. For example, I found a sentence he said when he was three years old. "I want a 'fear shield'... something to stop me from being afraid." When he was five, he asked me whether, when we fly in a plane, we can reach God and added, "I wish that one day our whole family could fly and reach God together." So why didn't I take more notice of this sentence? I have so many regrets when I think of all the little things that happened and that he said.

In the first year I spent a lot of time soul searching and questioning... what did I do, what did I say, what didn't I say...? My husband was both in shock over what had happened, and at the same time it didn't quite register. He kept repeating over and over, "I don't believe it, I can't believe it." But he also wanted to return to some kind of normal life, to travel, to go to movies; he went back to working full-time quite soon after. Our lives seemed to flow in separate directions. But that was ok. He went to Africa, India, China – and I stayed home.

A year after it happened, my mother had a complete nervous breakdown. She simply couldn't accept that her grandson had committed suicide and the magnitude of the tragedy was too great for her. She just couldn't cope. She is still alive, but has sunk into deep depression. My mother-in-law showed no external signs, she didn't talk about it at all, but she became totally withdrawn, as if a door had been bolted shut. In families there are no set rules for coping.

We have relatives who are willing to listen and talk, but most of them just want to get on with their lives. They're not interested in coming to the memorial services; they don't want to be confronted by the sadness. After it happened to us, we suddenly realized how widespread the phenomenon was. Suddenly we saw articles in the newspaper, things that previously we had not taken notice of. Different people started telling us that in their family there had been a suicide, a father, mother, or brother, and it happened to them when there were no support groups for victims of suicide, people didn't tell anyone about what had happened in their families, and in general there was relatively little discussion of suicide. The truth is that now when I look back, on one level, I still can't believe that it happened to us. Actually I can't understand how I survived the years since it happened, although in a sense I don't really 'live'. Death constantly surrounds me. How much time do I have left to live? It's just a matter of time. I have reserved a burial plot next to him, so I know where I'll be.

My priorities have changed. I know that nothing is as it seems. Many things that I once considered important have lost their value. They're just not worth that much, not success, not money, and not entertainment.

My relationship with my other children, with his siblings, has on the one hand really strengthened. But on the other hand I have doubts about the quality of my mothering. What sort of a mother am I for them? It's important for me that they're alright. I regret so much that they had to experience such a terrible tragedy, one which will definitely scar them for the rest of their lives. In a way, our daughter became a kind of parent to us. For instance, she bought me clothes. She understood that I wouldn't go out and buy myself clothes, so she did it for me. Our son won't talk about the tragedy at all. As if it didn't happen. When he talks about his childhood he never talks about his brother, as if he never existed. He only talks about himself and his sister. He comes to the memorial services. He has withdrawn, become totally introverted. But when he hears about a suicide, especially of a young person, he calls us and says: "Someone committed suicide, perhaps you should go and try to help the parents!" When we joined the support group for parents, our daughter established a support group for siblings. But our son wouldn't join it.

At a certain stage, I stopped going to our therapist. I started to suffer from excruciating headaches, and I felt that I needed help. I approached the leader of our support group (who had meanwhile ceased to lead the group), and I met with him for almost two years. He helped me to dismantle the 'time-bomb of guilt' I was carrying around. He used to tell me, "Wait, think... if you had behaved differently, do you think you could have prevented his suicide?" Gradually I came to realize that there is a limit to the amount that I am to blame, and I began to understand that I can't control everything that happens.

I thought about how I would react if, for example, my father had committed suicide when I was nine years old, the age you (*the interviewer*) were at your father's suicide. It would have totally destroyed me. Perhaps I couldn't have coped at all, and then the next question is: "Which of the tragedies is greater?" Today I am able to cope, I go to work... however as a child, what resources would I have had? People experience terrible things that are not their fault, who knows what is more difficult.

Because of my headaches I was referred to a psychiatrist. I told him about Daniel, and after about 10 minutes he described the following scenario. He said that it wasn't a passing crisis for Daniel, but rather the beginning of a process that could have gone on for many years and caused him a great deal of suffering. He claimed that Daniel became aware of the seriousness of his situation and decided to spare himself, and us, from the suffering. He said: "Be thankful that he had eighteen good years, there are kids who drag things like this on into their twenties and thirties, and then decide to end their lives. At that point the result of their suicide is much more complicated and far more destructive, since the family has already suffered for a long time." It was hard for me to hear this. I told him: "You didn't know him", but he said that this happens to many young men at that age. He asked me why I never took sleeping pills, to which I replied that I never took them because I wanted to suffer. So he didn't even prescribe any pills for depression and anxiety for me. I still suffer from headaches.

I told a friend of mine, whose son also committed suicide, what my psychiatrist had said and she was furious with him. She said that in her opinion it's not true to say that if there is some kind of crisis in one's life, it has to end in suicide. From a professional point of view she knows that if there is timely, and appropriate intervention, prevention is possible. It's true that in their case they did everything possible, and nothing helped, but she believes that it is possible to prevent the final step. I don't know if the psychiatrist was right or not, but at the time, after meeting with him I felt that the things he said calmed me down. It appeared that he was telling me that I was not to blame and that it would have been very difficult to prevent Daniel's suicide – that it was inevitable.

On the other hand, how is it possible to differentiate between a son's personality and the type of mothering he experienced? Didn't we grow up believing in the theory of the importance of the connection between mother and child, on the importance of the early years of life, on 'quality time'? So what happened here? What went wrong? What really hurts is that he was such a cute child...such a contented, happy, funny, child, and unbelievably sweet. It's frightening! We wanted him so much, the pregnancy was easy, the birth was smooth, he had no developmental problems, no behavioral problems, no learning problems, and he rarely rebelled even as a teenager. Our family was stable, conservative, nothing was lacking, nothing seemed to be wrong. It is so frightening. It's hard to talk about an eighteen year old's personality. It wasn't yet fully formed.

When he was about two or three years old, if the peas on his plate touched the rice, he would throw his plate down in anger. After the tragedy, his sister speculated that perhaps the crisis involved his enlistment into the military, and his reaction might have been something like taking the plate and throwing it. But in this case the plate was his life. And ours, too.

The army gave us his file. One of the things we found was a questionnaire he was asked to complete during his recruitment process. In it was the question, what are your good qualities. And what did he write? "I am stable and rational." In math, there is only one solution to a problem. There are no 'maybe' solutions. Perhaps this is connected to some kind of view of reality...black or white, yes or no.

Our lives changed completely. When I walk in the street I can feel the reflection of my own preconceived ideas in others. I think that they are thinking, "Here is the woman whose son committed suicide." I hear the question that they don't ask me (in fact sometimes I do get asked): "How can you go on living?" I don't tell everyone what happened. It's not easy to utter the word 'suicide'. Often, when people ask me what happened I say, "Not now, we'll talk about it some other time." It's especially difficult for me when I meet mothers who love their role as mothers and feel like they are really great mothers. This is where I feel like a failure.

Yesterday in the house I found the book, How to talk to your teenage son. We have always had it. When Daniel reached puberty I thought of reading it for the third time but then I thought that there was no need. Obviously today I think that perhaps if I had read it...

Yesterday I wrote a story about him. You know what's great about literature? That there's an end to the plot, and all the loose threads come together. But in real life it's different. The threads remain unraveled. Nothing can tie them together. The plot remains unresolved and no matter what happens this story will never have a happy ending.

Sandra

I'm 55 years old. What would you like to know about me? I grew up in a regular family. My parents were Zionists. Both my brother and I went to live on kibbutz, but we left and moved to the city. We didn't like communal living, and I didn't like the system of education, the communal sleeping arrangements in the children's houses, and all this became an open wound after what happened.

I felt that this type of life style did not suit us, but I didn't do a thing about it, I just went along thinking that perhaps it was ok, but in time, I realized that for us it wasn't ok. A large part of my guilt is buried there. We left, at first for a trial period, but very quickly we realized that we would never return to the kibbutz.

The next stage of my life began with my husband and me moving to live in the city, managing on our own, raising children, finding work... and then one day Sarah, our daughter, committed suicide. This was the most out of character thing that could have happened, that had ever happened and has ever happened to us to this day. Her suicide was so unexpected from any and every point of view, for us and for everyone else. There wasn't a single person who said that there were signs.

Everyone who knew her was in shock, just as we were. There were no signs of depression of any kind, and I personally don't really believe that she was depressed. There was nothing. There had however been other suicides in the family: my husband's mother committed suicide. She nursed her own mother who was sick, and she always said that she never wanted to get old. And that's exactly what happened. When she found out that she had cancer, her husband warned us that she was talking about committing suicide. Sarah never knew her grandmother but she had heard the story. At first, we just said that her grandmother had died, but at some stage we told her that it was suicide. I have to admit that I really loved my mother-in-law. She was a very special, amazing woman and we understood one another. I wasn't angry with her and perhaps at some level I sent a message of empathy with the act. I never said that it was a terrible thing. Sarah grew up with this story and in her suicide note she wrote, "Perhaps I'm just like my grandmother." I think there must be some connection.

Sarah was a headstrong child, a real powerhouse. She was already politically active at 15. She had a friend who committed suicide. I only found out about this much later. When it happened she mentioned something, and

I, foolishly, didn't take very much notice and didn't discuss it with her. She seemed to take this "lack of interest" to mean that it's not so terrible to do this. She hated school and always fantasized that she was somewhere else. Even though she had lots of friends and they were always at our place, she saw herself as a loner, and as not having a circle of friends. That's how she saw herself.

But somewhere deep inside I still don't believe that her suicide was connected to experiences she had gone through. It was something more than this. At first, after the tragedy, one of the psychologists said that it appeared from her suicide note that there was some 'other force acting upon her'. When she was born she cried incessantly, and it seemed as if she didn't want to be born, she was born almost one month late. In hindsight it felt as if she didn't want to come into this world. I have gone through various stages since her suicide and at each stage I have reached a different understanding. Twelve years have gone by and these thoughts are part of where I have been, what I have understood, the questions I have asked...where, why, and for what?!

Of course it bothers me when I think of the mistakes I might have made. Why didn't I spend more time with her, why didn't I try to engage her in more meaningful conversations when she was having problems at school? I could write a book about everything I *didn't* do. As the years have gone by I see that there are plenty of parents who have done worse things than I did, and their kids are still alive, but thoughts like these don't really make it easier for me. How does one go on? How does one go on living? But when it happened we still had two other little children. They were like two frightened little chicks. My son Mark said something really wise soon after it happened "... so what now... are we never going to laugh again?" Does this mean our lives are over? We realized that the children deserve to live full lives and not live forever under the cloud of the trauma. We even dared to say that we deserve to live. At first we forced ourselves to smile... I don't mean to put an artificial smile on our faces, but we went back to try living a normal life... which means that we didn't spend all our time talking about what had happened.

We didn't hide it, we cried when we were alone. There was the funeral and then there were the memorial services, but the boys didn't want to talk about her very much, they said that if they wanted to talk they would ask questions. So that's how our routine returned to 'normal'; and we made sure to give the boys everything they would have had, had this not occurred. We made an effort to return to normal and I think that to a great extent we succeeded. It wasn't easy to attend parent-teacher meetings at the same school, to climb Masada again on a school trip, the way we had done with her. The children knew we were suffering, but we made every effort to have a normal life.

I am confronted with the tragedy countless times every day, but every day the length of time when I don't think about the tragedy gets longer. This change became most obvious when I joined a support group. This was the first time I had met others who had gone through a similar experience. I saw that there were other people 'normal', 'regular' people to whom this had happened. Until then I was convinced that I was a terrible mother.

I have always lacked self-confidence, so when she committed suicide it really knocked me out. Today I am able to control my feelings, can make up my mind to think about Sarah, allow myself to be engulfed in sadness, and then choose to leave the sadness behind and enjoy what I have now. Of course there are surprises along the way, things that suddenly remind me of her, like seeing one of her girlfriends in the street, and if she's wheeling a baby, then it is even harder to cope... and then it's receiving wedding invitations. I can't say that I am happy, but I am able to enjoy things. We go overseas and I enjoy that; of course Sarah is there with us, she's with us all the time, but I am able to separate and this is due to the enormous effort we have made, especially for the children.

Sometimes I look back and feel that I was critical, demanding, and not a good mother. So I say to myself, ok, but you didn't know any other way! I also grew up in a family where sharing and discussion were not encouraged.

Sarah committed suicide when her friends were away. She wrote a letter to one of her friends: "I already miss you. When you come back something terrible will have happened."

We arrived home after being told that something terrible had happened. We were sure there had been an accident. Then the police investigator approached and asked us if she had been depressed. Sarah? Depressed? No way! What happened? But we already understood that if she wanted to commit suicide, she would do it. There were no limits to her determination, her strength. I'm sure that she thought she'd be looking down on us from above. She planned her funeral and I'm sure she imagined that she'd be able to see it. This is the age when kids think about the meaning of life, and I'm sure that in their circle of friends they talked about suicide, but Sarah was the only one who went and did it.

What makes up our daily lives, apart from nostalgia, sadness, pain, longing, and some guilt feelings? But with all of my feelings of guilt, and I do admit that I might have made some mistakes, it is clear to me that her decision to commit suicide did not result from my behavior, and understanding this has been a great help; even in the support group, hearing about the incidents that other parents regretted and thought might have influenced their children, made me realize how ridiculous, even insignificant are the things that people regretted doing. So it became clear to me that her suicide was not my fault. On the other hand, I still can't say this with a totally clear conscience. A part of me blames myself for not setting the scene for her to talk, if I had encouraged her to talk, everything may have been different, and perhaps she would have found a way to ask for help. But this feeling of mine is gradually fading. And since the feeling that it was 'she' and not 'me' grows, so too, the feeling of relief grows.

Today her suicide is not something I talk about. At first I was surrounded by people who knew what had happened. Even today I meet some people who tell me that they remember what happened. But now when I meet new people I don't bother to tell them what happened. Even at the clinic, for example, when they ask me how many children I have, even though it's very difficult, I just say two. This process took a long time.

The hardest thing now is that if I did this to one of my children, what kind of mother am I, what kind of parents are we, and how do we continue to raise our other children? When Sarah was still alive, I relied on my instincts and intuition. I have intuition and on that basis I thought I could raise my children. But since that shocking blow, I questioned how to go on, what to do now? What did we do wrong? And what do we do now? We felt that if the path we had taken till now was not the correct one, what path should we take? But the psychologist who we have been seeing helped us understand that we were not bad parents and that we could continue raising our children in the same way. And so we go on.

My husband says that guilt is a deep hole and he's not prepared to fall into it. He goes to her grave twice a week to look after the plants; he and I talk about Sarah, but not about the effect that her suicide has had on him. He's not prepared to talk about that. It is even harder for my mother to understand it. I think it's twice as hard for her... she is grieving for her granddaughter and also for the pain her own daughter is going through. That grief is hard to contain.

Sometimes I'm overcome with jealousy when I meet people whose lives are normal and to whom nothing bad has ever happened. We have friends who have four girls, *four girls*... do you know what that means for me? It's hard for me to cope. It's true we have two lovely happy, healthy children but there's a giant hole. I can also only talk about my jealousy in the support group where I can air all my 'bad' feelings.

The other thing that has happened is that I have started to believe in all kinds of mystical signs and coincidences. A short time before it happened I was in a taxi with a driver who asked me how many children I had. I told him, "… three and that's all I want." Soon after that conversation the tragedy occurred. Don't you think I tempted fate? I don't remember the details of what I said but I feel that those few foolish words might have brought about this disaster.

Another thing is the anxiety that accompanies me as I raise my children. I don't have the luxury of saying, "It won't happen to me!" It has already happened to me, and it can happen, anything is possible, and that's really frightening. I didn't manage to control this so my children grew up with a hysterical and anxious mother. Even before it happened I wasn't exactly the calmest person, but after 'the event' if my children were more than half an hour late coming home from school, I immediately called all their friends parents. And this was before all the terrorist attacks… I would have loved it if they didn't want to go out on trips; who knows what and where something awful awaits us.

SUICIDE OF A SIBLING

A lison Wertheimer wrote her book "A Special Scar"[57] after her sister, aged 39 committed suicide leaving a husband, a nine year old girl, and a six year old boy. Her death was a total shock for Alison as it was the first time she had experienced a death of someone so close to her. In addition, she had nothing to compare the shock of the death of a loved one, to death by suicide. It took her some time to understand how different and much more difficult it is for the bereaved, when a family member commits suicide. The author notes that in the summer before she committed suicide, her sister had been admitted to a psychiatric hospital and was diagnosed with manic depression. The thought that her sister might take her own life never, however, occurred to Alison. She feels that she was denied the opportunity to say goodbye properly to her... and then it was too late.

Survivors, whose siblings committed suicide, have spoken with me of guilt and anger, as have other family members, but siblings' feelings often differ from those of other family members. There are feelings of shame and guilt for being the surviving sibling, sometimes feeling that the dead sibling may have been closer to the parents, may have been loved more, or perhaps was the more successful one. Then there is anger towards the dead sibling because the surviving sibling is unable to understand why they did it at all; why did they do this 'to me' (the surviving sibling); and anger because the surviving sibling must cope with all these challenging and painful issues.

In many of the interviews the attribute of 'perfectionism' arose. In many cases, the desire to achieve perfection, accompanied by difficulty to accept 'failure' was characteristic of the deceased. These qualities were often raised in interviews with families as part of an explanation or an attempt to understand the traits that characterize people who commit suicide.

---

57 Wertheimer, A. (1991). *A special Scar: The Experiences of People Bereaved by Suicide.*

In his book, which also deals with bereavement following suicide, Colin Pritchard [58] writes about the initial difficulties encountered by the surviving families, relating in particular to problems with which the surviving siblings must cope. While their sibling was alive, the survivors had to deal with the fact that their parents' attention was focused on the other sibling, if and when they suffered of anxiety or depression; and after the death, they must live with the never-ending grief in the family, which obviously diverts attention away from the surviving sibling.

Wertheimer stresses that the repercussions of this loss will remain with the surviving sibling as long as they live. The question often asked is whether this experience will weaken or strengthen the survivors.

Mark, whose interview appears in the next chapter, published a booklet in memory of his sister, on the tenth anniversary of her death. When she committed suicide at the age of sixteen, he was thirteen years old. He begins: "My sister Sarah was buried in two coffins. Her body was buried in a coffin in the cemetery, and her life was buried in a wooden cupboard in our living-room. For me, the cupboard in the living room was as much a coffin as the coffin in the cemetery. It was as if it was buried deep in the ground and I wouldn't dare get close to it."

He recalls that after her death he expressed the desire for his life to return to 'normal' as quickly as possible, and he wanted the rest of the family to do the same. This is probably one of the unique characteristics of grief following the suicide of a sibling: the feeling that their death has changed the nature and identity not only of the deceased, but also that of the whole family. While the parents are left with guilt feelings forever, siblings are labeled and given an identity of 'someone whose sibling committed suicide', an identity the survivor didn't choose. The death of a sibling irreversibly alters the surviving sibling's life.

From the interviews I conducted, I discovered that the birth order of siblings in the family is important in terms of the effect on the surviving sibling. If the survivor is older than the deceased, the surviving sibling tends to identify with the parents and adopt some of the burden of guilt, feeling that perhaps they didn't do enough to prevent the suicide, or were not attuned to any signs of distress. On the other hand, when surviving siblings are younger, they may not suffer from the same guilt feelings as older siblings, however they are very likely to be exposed to the parents' fears that they, too, may commit suicide, especially when they reach the same age that the deceased

58   Colin Pritchard (1996). *Suicide: the Ultimate Rejection?*

was when the suicide occurred. In both cases, the weight of this burden is oppressive and the suffering is long-lasting.

Mark

Sarah, Mark's sister and Sandra's daughter, committed suicide when Mark was thirteen years old. In a booklet Mark published in her memory, he tried to describe what she was like, from things she had written, and from details her friends and family could supply. Mark brings the booklet with him to our meeting.

I'm twenty-four years old and Sarah was my older sister. There were three of us; I have a younger brother. We grew up on kibbutz, and when I was about seven years old we moved here, to the city. Before she committed suicide I can't say that I really knew her. Today I can say that I didn't know her. The anniversary of her death will be in about a month. When she committed suicide she was sixteen and a half. There weren't really any warning signs because she was such a strong person. Perhaps in hindsight there was a sign here and there, but they were really just slips of the tongue. It wasn't really possible to pick anything up from these. She didn't tell anyone about her plan. She managed to keep it to herself really well. She stood on the railway tracks; I know that this idea was not original, she heard about it from other people.

After it happened I ran away. I ran away from the funeral, and from the week of mourning, the 'Shiva'. I didn't think her suicide had anything to do with me and I didn't want any connection to the whole thing. I was afraid that my parents would start behaving differently.

The first question I asked my parents when we were at the hospital (Sarah was still in the hospital for a day) was, "Can we smile again?" That was the first thing that worried me. And so life went on until one year before I was recruited into the army. We didn't talk about her at home. My parents preferred not to, or didn't know how, to speak about her. I didn't want to talk, and my little brother followed my example. We had a small cupboard in the house which was full of her things, and her books were organized neatly on top of it. I didn't like to embarrass people by saying that my sister committed suicide. If anyone asked about my sister, I used to just say that she died.

It places me in a dilemma, whenever anyone asks me how many siblings I have. Usually I say, "... one." Only after many years was I able to say that my sister committed suicide. I think it made the person asking feel uncomfortable, and also, what does it say about me. Maybe it will happen to me, too?

A year before I went into the army I decided to find out more about my sister. I think this had to do with my maturing, and because I was about to graduate from school. I became more interested in her. The first thing I did was to examine how it affected *me*. This also made me feel guilty because I was using her suicide for my own personal needs, to see what was going on in my life. At first I felt that what she did had nothing to do with me, and had no effect on me, and here suddenly, I was using it. For instance in the army, because of what she had done, I was able to serve as a trainer in a combat unit, and did not have to serve in actual combat. Then I felt guilty that I was using her suicide to make my life easier, something which I had no right to do, after all - she was who she was, and I am who I am, yet despite it all I used the opportunity for my own means. I also 'used' this when I was in school. It happened just as I went up to 7th grade and I was put into a class that I didn't want to be in, so immediately after her suicide they asked me at school what I wanted. I said that I wanted to be put in a different class. Even then I felt as if I was taking advantage of her death and that wasn't really right.

My interest and curiosity about her, and the effect of her suicide, grew when I was in the army, but it still was not a major part of my life. I also think about the effect it had on my younger brother. The effect on him is more pronounced – he didn't talk about it for years. Only later were we more open about the whole event, although even today he isn't entirely comfortable talking about it.

After the army I had time on my hands and I decided to do something connected with Sarah. I wanted to find out who she was. I interviewed people, read things that she had written – she wrote prolifically considering that she was only sixteen years old. Last year, which was ten years after her death, I published this booklet about her. It helped people communicate more freely. After I gave copies of the booklet to the family members we had a meeting, and they talked for about two hours about things that hadn't been talked about for ten years. Since then the whole topic has become much more open, also with my parents. The booklet was very significant for me and also for my brother who was nine years old when Sarah committed suicide; he really didn't know her. The booklet and the meeting were very important.

While writing the booklet, and also from conversations with people, I was suddenly struck by an idea, a 'brainwave', that suicide is an 'active death'. It's not just that committing suicide is an 'intentional act', but people remain in a state of active unresolved questioning about the death, since there is always the question of why the person did it, and reservations about the suicide itself. I don't think these questions surround other forms of death. For instance if someone is killed in a car accident, or in the army, these questions don't arise. Not in this way.

Everyone I spoke to had their own opinion about why she did it. And I think that they are all actively involved with her even after her death, questioning and trying to understand why she did it. This active involvement causes memories of her to change. Recently we had a memorial service for my aunt, who was killed in a car accident. Everyone's memories of her were clear, and hadn't changed. They were the same for all of us. However in the case of Sarah, everyone's memories are different. If everyone who talked to me about her got together in the one room, their memories would differ. I think this has to do with the fact that memories of the deceased are shaped by one's own view of suicide. People still have a running dialog with Sarah about why she did it, even though she's no longer here. When I realized this, I related to the memories of her and to what people told me about her, with caution. I listened to what people had to say with reservations. For instance she had a drama teacher who she really loved. The teacher described Sarah as having blond hair, which was not at all true. But it was fascinating to hear what people had to say.

Even her friends were totally preoccupied and engrossed with her suicide. They disagreed with her, and these disagreements distorted their memories of her... and all I wanted was to get to know her. It's hard to get to know someone this way. I wrote and gradually I felt that the picture I was getting about Sarah was of a complete stranger. Another problem I encountered was that she lived her life from beginning to end, and she lived it in chronological order, however for me, the end was the beginning of my journey to get to know her. Therefore this booklet is not a totally accurate portrayal of her; rather it is how I met her, after ten years.

I can only guess at why she committed suicide. I disagreed with what the psychologist said. I asked him whether it was possible that she did the right thing for herself. She left a ten page letter written in small, tightly spaced handwriting, explaining why she wanted to take her life. According to the letter, she had decided that it was the most logical thing to do. On the other hand, everyone who talked about her was convinced that she was wrong. Again I asked him if for her, perhaps suicide was the right thing, because in my mind she was really clever, very mature, and I think that we should respect what she did because of this. Clearly *for me* personally, she made a mistake, but that doesn't mean that *for her* it was a mistake. I think that the very thought that suicide can be 'okay', is frightening in itself. I wrote at the end of the booklet, "It appears to me that Sarah was completely at peace with her decision." This sentence is not totally convincing, but it's comforting to see Sarah in this light, as she really was. To say that she was 'right' is of course frightening, because that means that there is a possibility that I could do the same thing?

I actually believed, or rather it was more an unconscious thought, that perhaps there was some family gene, a destructive gene, from the other side of the family, because my grandmother also committed suicide. She had cancer and she didn't want to become a burden; my aunt was killed in a car accident, and after that Sarah died. So I thought that in every generation in our family someone had suffered a 'violent' death.

If we go back to the question of why she committed suicide, she wrote in her suicide letter that she had lived a full life. But she was also interested to see what would happen if she committed suicide, "to be present at her own funeral." She often felt that it was difficult for her to communicate with others and she was never fully satisfied with the quality of the relationships she formed.

One year before she committed suicide, someone she knew also committed suicide and I think that really affected her. I'm not saying that we shouldn't talk about suicide, but I do think that if someone you know commits suicide, it's possible to see the act as 'plausible'. So after her friend's suicide, she began to make plans in that direction. She began to say goodbye to her friends, and they didn't even realize that she was doing so; she began to sever ties, so that people who knew her wouldn't get hurt. This was a constant internal struggle. She wrote about the struggle between the natural desire to make friends, and the desire to break ties.

I assume that someone who plans to commit suicide has guilt feelings knowing that they are going to hurt others. And later on the surviving relatives have guilt feelings; they blame themselves. They all feel guilty, but of course especially the parents. When a sixteen year old child commits suicide, obviously it destroys the parents' self-confidence. My parents often talked about this. There were two options, to accept suicide, or argue about it. Guilt is really a kind of argument. In her letter she wrote, "Do not blame yourselves, I'm responsible for this." And guilt is essentially a denial of what she said. My mother searched her soul trying to discover how she was to blame. What did she do differently than other mothers to cause this? Maybe because they (my parents) did not interfere in her life, gave her space... who knows...

Perhaps there is some semblance of comfort when someone commits suicide after suffering from depression, because the act puts an end to their misery. But my sister appeared to be so happy, surrounded by friends. So my parents were denied even this comfort. In a way I think that she wanted to commit suicide, but not to die; first to do it - and then to see what would be. This is why some people had the idea that she made a mistake, a mistake that was impossible to correct. There were no warning signs, however afterwards some of her friends analyzed things that had occurred. I think that she was totally at peace with her decision; and I think that even this knowledge is a source of comfort to the family, the siblings, and parents. However on the other hand you could say that she was only sixteen years old so what could she really know and understand, she didn't even get a chance to marry. The fact that she was at peace with her decision seems very significant to me. It appears from her letter, and also the way she committed suicide, that she felt that her decision was the correct one.

The main problem, and she didn't really address this, was what she did to our family by committing suicide. One good thing that came out of making the booklet was that it made my parents look beyond their own perceived guilt, and see that the whole story did not revolve only around them; there were also friends involved and this helped lessen their own feelings of guilt. She wrote that she knew that her suicide would have an effect, but she didn't want to hurt her parents. This is quite naïve, I think, to write to people "Don't blame yourselves." She should have known better than that, but possibly the urge to do it was stronger than she was.

She wrote letters. She also wrote to me; her letter to me was really advice for the future, a guide to life...when you grow up...

I think that there's a problem with suicides in the army because of easy access to weapons. For a year and a half my sister looked for a way to do it. When a soldier commits suicide, the thought always arises, if only he didn't have a gun, perhaps he would have thought about it once more and change his mind. This is one of the problems in the army and that's why there are so many suicides amongst soldiers. In the army there's a policy not to talk about suicide, and when it does happen, it is suppressed, as if it didn't happen. In any case, I don't think that, for instance, not being accepted to officer's training school is a reason to commit suicide. There must be something else. I can say for myself that when I was in the army I looked for signs in others, I wanted to make sure that I was doing all I could to detect any cues. I'm sure that this is connected to feelings of guilt. In fact there was one potential incident; I was constantly fearful that someone in my unit would decide to commit suicide and that I'd miss the signs. There was one soldier who I was sure that was going to harm himself; I told others close to him to watch over him, and take notice of any unusual behavior. In the end he was really grateful to me. I am always on the lookout and try to see where I can help. Obviously this is one way in which my sister's suicide affected me.

Kevin

Just over two years ago my brother committed suicide. He was in his twenties and there's no doubt that him doing this affected the whole family. I guess you could say we had some kind of warning, since he tried to commit suicide once before, and he talked about it. We knew he had problems and thought that something like this might happen so it wasn't a total surprise... but we still felt that we had been hit with a sledge hammer. Of course, we are always questioning whether we could have prevented it. But he left a letter in which he accepted full responsibility for what he did. This was of some comfort and help to us, especially for my parents. From what he wrote in his letter, he made it clear, and we understood, that life was really hard for him.

He loved sport, and played with his whole heart and soul. In fact he threw himself wholeheartedly into everything he did. Now in hindsight I see that this quality in and of itself was a problem; he was a person who would not compromise, a man of extremes, everything for him was black or white. He didn't understand how there could be people who would say one thing and do something else, people who cut corners. He followed the truth to the end, and only today do I realize that you just can't do this. He was unwavering in everything he did, and gave it his all; he wouldn't side-step at all. But you can't live life like this. Life is made up of compromises.

He was super intelligent and always asked probing questions, argued about the meaning of life, and questioned why we live at all; his arguments were often difficult to counter. He was hospitalized in the psychiatric ward, but the doctors couldn't find the right drug to help him. It was almost funny... he even managed to send his psychiatrist into a depression. The psychiatrist couldn't understand how someone so intelligent and talented would want to die. People who didn't know him very well couldn't see it. He had so many friends, went to parties; the first time he danced at a wedding was two weeks before he committed suicide. The first time he attempted suicide was when he was seventeen, then again when he was in the army, and the last time he succeeded. He managed to do it 'according to the book', attempt, warning, and execution. For sure it was worst for my parents. Even though we knew that one day it might happen, there was always the hope that he would pull out of it. He had a girlfriend who knew everything about him, and there wasn't another person alive who could pull him out of it. He had everything, talent, friends, he knew how to get things done, how to get people to do things that needed to be done... but he had no desire to live.

In my opinion he should have been medicated, however the doctors in the psychiatric ward couldn't find any drugs which could help him. There's no doubt that he definitely needed medication. We could see in his eyes that he was suffering, and I'm not sure that we helped as much as we could have. We could see that he was actually suffering physically. When he finished his basic training in the army, I remember seeing the suffering in his eyes. The fact that he was such an intelligent person who was always thinking about the meaning of life, that he had so much time to think, together with his genetic makeup, and his black and white extreme outlook on life was a fatal combination which in my opinion could lead anyone to commit suicide. I think he could have received more medical help, perhaps today they know more.

Although we really tried, there is always the feeling that we could have done more. I'm sure that therapy with a psychologist could not have helped him. It was not a classic case of an intelligent person sitting across from you. He was someone who had good social skills, interacted well, and when he sat in front of you he could logically explain why it was not worth living. I believe that in this situation only drugs can help such a person. Perhaps the correct thing would have been to send him to places that deal with the meaning of life, perhaps through religion; this thought has occurred to me just now.

Because we thought that this could happen, the element of total shock was not there. Towards the end he had totally exhausted the family. Today I think that he planned every step, preparing the groundwork just like in the army, just so he would be left alone. He had put a lot of thought into the letter he left; it was obvious that it was carefully thought out, not written on impulse. The letter was structured and beautifully written, and there was considerable consolation in that it was obvious he had planned the whole thing to the end; in the letter he totally removed all responsibility from the family. He wrote, "This is life, each person chooses what to do with their life, and I chose not to continue, to take responsibility for my own actions ... none of this is to do with you, my family."

There are some families who say if only the person would have talked, if only we had known, perhaps we could have helped; but in our case he spoke, and we still couldn't prevent it. They say first there is shock, then anger, and then the routine of life returns, but it's not like that. There's always the nagging thought that perhaps we could have done something differently. He wrote, "If you cry, you cry for yourselves, don't cry for me because I am not suffering anymore." But when he was suffering at home there was still some hope. There may have been a reason to go on; after all, suffering is part of life, especially when it concerns someone so young who has his whole life ahead of him. Perhaps if he had gone on and done something with his life, things could have turned out differently.

On the other hand, there are always two sides to every story. In Israel there are over three hundred suicides a year, about one a day, and with suicide you can't even talk about 'the will of God' which leaves the family with the feeling that in spite of everything maybe it would have been possible to do more. When someone dies in a war, of course the pain is unfathomable, but the family does not have the thoughts that haunt ('haunt' is an understatement) the family after a suicide, about if and how it could have been prevented. These thoughts and the thought that their death was unnecessary are terrible. However in my brother's case I'm sure that he was sick, and they couldn't find the right medication for him.

He was the total opposite of an egoist. He had absolutely no intention of showing us how sorry we would be. In fact the opposite was true. He parted from everyone in order to make it easier for them.

I think that going back to their jobs and working was very good for my parents. They appear to function really well, both at work and at home. Of course the memorial services and going to the cemetery are really difficult for all of us. At the cemetery we always repeat what he said, like a mantra, "If you cry, you cry for yourselves, don't cry for me because I am not suffering anymore." But everything is not as it seems. Everyone thinks that my mother is fine, but this is just how it appears on the surface. Inside there's a void. I know that sometimes she can't understand how she goes on, how she continues to live.

Perhaps they should bring counselors to the schools. There's a real need for counseling for teenagers, even if it's to make them aware that there is medication available. It's better to take medication... if it isn't suitable, you can always stop. At least problems should be addressed at an early stage. But it's hard to talk about medication because sometimes you're talking about mental illness and there's still a stigma attached to anything to do with psychiatric problems.

There's something else I want to say about the pain. It doesn't disappear, it may not be as acute, but it just gets deeper. It seeps in further and further. It's not about a raw nerve any more, when you touch the nerve I don't go to pieces, but with time, the magnitude of the tragedy sinks in. You don't realize at first that you only have one chance at life, and how much it hurts that someone who had so much to give, to contribute, is gone. In time you realize, even when you're being rational, how tragic it is.

I WISH HE HAD DIED IN A WAR:
THE HIERARCHY OF BEREAVEMENT

During the interviews I conducted, I have heard the same feelings and experiences repeated over and over: common fears, anxieties, ways of dealing and coping with them, all similar versions of different people's stories. One particular sentence which kept recurring most often was, "I wish he had died in a war."

When the comparison is made between the death of someone by suicide and death in a war, dying in a war is considered 'a better way to die' since unlike suicide, death as a result of war does not contravene human nature, and is not a death in vain. Respect is bestowed upon the family in its hour of grief and continues well into the future. While all loss is tragic, if a family is to lose one of its members, from the family's point of view, death in a war is 'preferable'. The bereaved family becomes part of a societal group, a unique collective body known as 'the Family of the Bereaved', whereas the families of people who commit suicide have no formal status in society. Soldiers who die in battle fall in the service of their country, thus making their death a heroic one and they are remembered and respected as brave and honorable, while people, who commit suicide, are at the other end of the pride and shame spectrum of circumstances associated with their death. Therefore not only is the manner of their death obscured, but so too is the person who committed suicide, along with any memory of them[59]. In this context Roz says: "I thought to myself, if he had to die, why didn't he die in a war? This would have made his death heroic, rather than shameful..." and as Rachel said about her husband "If he was to die, it would have been better

---

59 Avrami, S. (2009). The hierarchy of bereavement in Israel – war victims, terror victims and suicide survivors. In: L. Sher and A. Vilens (eds.). *Terror and Suicide*. NY: Nova Science Publishers.

had he had died in battle." The circumstances surrounding the death of a family member have meaning for the surviving family not only in the way they mourn but also for the social status the death creates for the survivors.

Suicide has a cultural aspect, and social and cultural implications: different societies deal with it in various ways. In ancient Greece it was considered a legitimate solution for existential problems; in Japan, hara-kiri was a form of self-execution aimed to avoid shame or humiliation for a deed which may bring dishonor or disgrace. With the emergence of Christianity, suicide was forbidden, just as it has always been in Judaism and as a result, in Jewish tradition, people who commit suicide are buried at the perimeter of the cemetery.

In both sociology and psychology, research has shown that society views the manner of death in a hierarchical manner. At the 'top' of the hierarchy are those who have fallen in war. In his book *Pain Unbound*[60] Israel Orbach relates the story of a woman whose husband committed suicide, but she tells everybody that he died in 1973, so people would assume that he had died during the Yom Kippur war, which occurred in that year. The writer and researcher Ruvik Rosenthal, whose brother died in that war, focuses his book *Is Bereavement Dead?*[61] on the claim that the perception of dying in the war as 'preferable' has weakened over the years, but writes that "A boy whose father died in a war saw him as a hero and a legend... and although the boy suffered a great loss, at the same time his father died an honorable death and this was something that sustained the boy as he matured: his father was a hero, someone whose death was meaningful." (p. 84-85).

In his book *Lovely Lady*[62] Yehonatan Gefen makes the point that "'suicide' was a dirty word in our parents' generation, in the land of heroes, unless of course you committed suicide for a national cause." This generation's dream was, according to Gefen, that if they were captured, and if the Syrians tortured them in order to get military secrets, then they would be able to commit suicide honorably. This supports the theory that not only is there a hierarchy of causes of death (where suicide is generally at the bottom), but there is also a hierarchy for different types of suicides – there are those which have heroic justification, transforming the deed into one that society can justify and accept. The national or military context changes the nature of the suicide to an act which becomes comprehensible, and therefore more easily

60 Israel Orbach, *Pain Unbound* (2000). Jerusalem: Schoken
61 Rubik Rosental, *Is Bereavement Dead?* (2001). Jerusalem: Keter
62 Yehonatan Gefen, *Lovely Lady* (1999). Tel Aviv: Dvir

sanctioned by friends and family.

The Masada narrative relates that the warriors on top of the Masada Mountain in the Judean desert, carried out a mass suicide so that they would not fall into the hands of the Romans, thereby not becoming prisoners of war. Generations of young Israelis have been raised on this story, and high school trips, and swearing in military ceremonies have taken place on top of that very mountain for decades. This retelling lauds suicide as an honorable solution for the warriors on the mountain in order to prevent the humiliation of captivity. In his book *Masada*[63] the archeologist Yigael Yadin wrote that the warriors had only two choices: surrender or death, and the leader of the uprising, Elazar Ben-Yair, decided that death was the preferred choice, rather than the humiliation of defeat and enslavement.

After two of his sons committed suicide, one of them during his military service, Tuvia Navot wrote his book *Do not Raise Your Hand*, referring to the biblical binding of Isaac by his father Abraham. [64] In his book, he discusses the hierarchy of dying, and ranks the ways in which the deaths occurred. This then determines whether the deceased will be remembered as a hero, or not. At one end of society's bereavement hierarchy are army casualties and at the other end are circumstances not connected to battle thereby placing them lower down. The status of soldiers who commit suicide during military service are located at the lowest end. In Israel a soldier who has committed suicide is buried inside a military graveyard, not by the fence.

In the book *Stone for a Stone* [65] there is a section which relates to the standard form for military headstones: 'Fell in battle'; 'Died in a military training accident', 'Fell during service', including illness or suicide.

Tuvia Navot also talks about death in battle, as the death of someone who did not 'simply die'. Similarly Saul, in the following interview, relates that after his father fell in battle during the war of independence, 'He didn't just die'... he was a hero". Following Saul's father's death, Saul's mother committed suicide. It was clear to Saul that the fact that his mother committed suicide following her husband's death in battle made her suicide honorable.

---

63 Yigael Yadin, *Masada* (1966). Tel Aviv and Haifa: Maariv and Shikmona
64 Tuvia Navot, *Do not raise your hand* (1996). Tel Aviv: ministry of defense publication
65 Batya Gur, *A Stone Under a Stone* (1998). Jerusalem: Keter

Saul

Saul was raised in his uncle's home after his father fell during the Israeli War of Independence, in 1948. He was six months old when his father was killed. His mother committed suicide about one year later. Researchers have observed that modern society still has preconceived ideas about war widows, thereby stigmatizing and labeling them, casting them into the role of victim. A widow who distances herself from her husband's memory or from his family is seen as betraying the nation, as well as the family of the fallen.

Today I am fifty-two years old. My mother committed suicide almost fifty years ago. I don't remember my parents. I had two mothers, my biological mother, and the 'mother' who raised me. I grew up in my mother's brother's home, and was raised by my uncle and his wife. This was quite normal for me, until I was ten years old when my family history was related to me, and they only did this because the story of my family appeared in the newspapers.

I'm not someone who talks a lot. In my home we talk but we don't cry... my daughter is the only one who talks and expresses her emotions; she's different than the rest of us.

When I look back, I think that the suicide seriously affected my self-confidence. I could have made more of myself but I didn't. I hold a senior position, but I believe I could have gone a lot further in my professional career. Although I'm successful I don't feel confident enough to demand what I feel I deserve. The suicide also affected my relationships with women.

I was always the best at everything I did, sports, studies, air-force training... I think I was always trying to prove something, but I wasn't really conscious of this at the time.

Do you know why she committed suicide? Did anyone tell you?

I don't know why she did it, I can only guess. They were a young, good looking couple living in a small community, on kibbutz, and she just couldn't see how she could go on alone. There were also prejudices... she couldn't form a relationship with another man after her husband was killed. Everyone on the kibbutz was very young and all their parents were holocaust survivors. Imagine, a kibbutz with no grandparents... so who had time for my mother and her problems? Who could have noticed one poor suffering soul in their midst? Everyone there had suffered and had their own problems. Of course I don't remember any of this.

I think something similar happened to me during the Yom Kippur war. I was a prisoner of war as a pilot in Egypt, and when I returned I was notified of friends who had been killed, one after the other. Everyone was dead. I can't even recall what happened to me when I was a prisoner – I just can't remember. Perhaps my childhood memories have similarly been erased.

It's possible that my experience is different from others. I have no guilt feelings whatsoever regarding my mother's suicide. Since my father was killed in a war, he didn't 'just die'... he was a hero, and therefore, she was his heroine. On the kibbutz they admired what she did; as if it was honorable of her to follow in his footsteps.

The whole world surrounding my parents disappeared. There are no photos, no names, no relatives... only after many years did I begin searching for my roots. In fact I am still searching.

Roz

I'm twenty eight years old. My father committed suicide when my mother was pregnant with me, so I never knew him; I also never knew how he died. On my fifteenth birthday my mother said that I was old enough to know that my father had committed suicide. She told me, and then she walked out of the room. After that we each went on with our own life. That's how I remember it today, but I'm not sure that this is the way it was. I don't remember the words she used. I assume that she said, "He killed himself..." but I don't remember for sure.

After that I felt alone in the world. I couldn't talk about my father with anyone. The first time I had thoughts of talking to anyone else about it was in high school. Before that, I just couldn't. Before I went into the army I went to visit my brother who lives overseas. I tried to talk to him about what had happened to our father, but that failed. I looked for opportunities to talk but the words just wouldn't come out of my mouth. I got the feeling that my brother really didn't want to talk about it.

From the minute I found out that my father had committed suicide, I was afraid. What if I was forced to talk about him? Somehow I managed to get the message across that I didn't want to talk about him, that this topic was off limits. When I finally did decide to talk, it was important to me that my close friends knew the truth. Whenever I felt that someone was close to me, I wanted them to know. But even then I only related the cold hard facts, nothing more than that. When I had a boyfriend, I knew for sure that I would tell him. But I don't even remember how I told him... how and what.

It turns out that there are more cases 'like mine'. I have a girlfriend who told me that she knows a girl whose mother committed suicide, and they don't talk about it with anyone. She said that when that girl told her boyfriend, he broke up with her.

When I began my university studies, I decided to go to therapy. I wanted to understand why I hadn't talked about it with my friends in high school. Through therapy I understood that I had been in shock from the revelation, and maybe I was afraid to talk about it because I had a feeling it was my fault. Suddenly I realized what I was afraid of. If it was my fault, what could I do about it? Also commit suicide? After a while I stopped going to the therapist. She wasn't very good for me. When it was difficult for me to talk about my father, I would change the topic and talk about other things ... but I really want to talk about him and his suicide. It's always lurking in the background and until I can open up and talk about it, it will continue to haunt me. I need someone who can help me verbalize my thoughts and feelings. It's important that people hear the facts from me, which is weird since up to now I know I have given the impression that I want to be left alone. Therefore no-one has dared to talk to me about it. I told someone at work and she found it unbelievable that twenty eight years later I still feel guilty, just like in the books. I don't know how he killed himself. I haven't asked. I don't have the strength to deal with the details.

Today, if I'm asked, I am able to say that he committed suicide, and that is something I couldn't say a while ago. Nevertheless I try to steer clear of the subject. It's exhausting to deal with it. Everyone knows but it's buried so deep and no-one is able to talk about it. The interesting thing is that everyone knew what happened, and only we think that it's such a huge secret. Suicide is something that everyone is ashamed of because 'good people don't do things like that'! I have often thought that if he had to die, why not in a war, in some heroic way, and not in such a shameful way.

At a certain stage, my feelings changed to anger, I couldn't understand why he chose to die before I was born. Didn't he want to know me? Today I care less; so what... I didn't know him, what he was like really means nothing to me. This week, I refused to go to his grave for the memorial service. I decided that I don't have to pretend any more...

I didn't know him, I never heard anything about him, and there were never any photos of him around the house. It's too bad I didn't know him, but today I feel that it's too late. Just like having a grandfather who died before you were born and you didn't know him except with grandfathers there are usually photos and stories. If he had been part of my childhood, I'm sure I'd feel differently. When I was ten years old my mother decided to stop having memorial services for him; I was sorry because I used to miss a day of school for the memorial service... I can't recall what happened at the services because no one really talked to me, but I didn't feel that there was anything unusual. I guess that's because I never asked how he died. Before my mother told me (when I was fifteen years old), I never knew that he had committed suicide. But when she told me, it was as if I had been waiting to be told. I think that perhaps the very fact that we never talked about him gave me the feeling that there was something unusual and problematic, surrounding the circumstances of his death. When I was little I sometimes thought that the door might open and he'd suddenly appear. I called my big brother 'dad', and my mother would say he's your brother, not your father. I didn't really want him to be my father, but sometimes I did want my mother to marry so I would have a father. I really wanted to call someone 'dad'.

Occasionally I had thoughts that it's all a dream and he's really not dead, or that something else happened, or else maybe he did die a hero's death. However, once I knew, the hardest thing was the 'secret', and the shame. Death is not something to be ashamed of, but suicide is. Somehow the underlying message I received at home was shame... but about what? No-one talked about that. There was just something in the air that we were ashamed of. Even today, it's hard for me to talk about it. It's as if part of me doesn't exist. In general, in my everyday life I'm a curious person, but when it comes to anything related to my father the urge to repress anything concerning him is greater than my curiosity about him. I believe that my mother didn't talk about it in order to protect me. Perhaps she was angry with him and felt that he ruined her life.

She said that she didn't want to make things any more difficult for us than they already were. I'm sure she had the best of intentions. The result of course is that I really know very little about him... but I'm ok with this.

My biggest fear is that there might be a genetic aspect, and it may be hereditary. This really bothers me. Maybe there's something in our family... perhaps I keep busy all the time so I won't have any free time for these fears to overwhelm me. I'm constantly busy, afraid of what might happen if I have too much time on my hands, afraid that it will happen to me too? Although I know I did nothing wrong, I still have the feeling that I had something to do with his suicide. Perhaps I choose to do so many things because I want to prove that I'm a success, to prove that I'm my own person, that I'm mentally stable and healthy. I'm a perfectionist and have always felt that I had to be perfect, to please everyone... show that I'm fine, that I won't cause any problems or do anything crazy. I sometimes feel that something in my personality may be lacking because I was raised only by my mother, and am lacking the influence of a father, although I do have his genes!

When I tell people what happened, they don't really know how to react. I used to worry about what they'd say. If it's something familial, then that includes me. When you share your story, the people you tell are automatically caught in the 'trap' and often don't know how to respond. The actual word 'suicide' has such powerful meaning for me that I can barely get the word out of my mouth, saying it is unbearable. I often wonder if, after hearing my story, people who are close to me distance themselves. I don't think people have really changed in their attitudes to suicide. When I was first told, I didn't know how to cope with the story; I felt as if part of my life had been destroyed.

That's why marriage is so important to me – as if, hey, here I have a family of my own, a normal family, something new, and it's mine! Now I am responsible for my own life. I have built a much more open family, one in which we talk about everything. Suicide is not something that everyone experiences. If there was one thing I tried to avoid, it was self-pity. Trying to hide this secret so no one would find out, so no-one would question me, took so much energy. I harbored this secret for twenty seven years ...so no one would find out. But now that I'm married, I'm at a different stage.

I read an article which said that the things that happen in the first few months of life affect a person for the rest of their life. This really worried me. But I'm only going to delve if there's someone who can help me; I'll only do this in therapy.

I don't think I have ever stopped grieving. My grief is something separate from the rest of my emotions. In therapy I understood that you have to dig really deeply to understand. I think that when I finally get in touch with my deepest emotions only then will I be able to say that I can live in peace with the fact that my father committed suicide; I still can't say that today.

Today, I can talk about it, but talking doesn't reflect my feelings, because acknowledging my feelings is very threatening. That's what happens when you live with a secret for twenty seven years. I can't even talk to myself about it! To lose one's father in a war is totally different. One's emotions are clearer and more defined. The more I think about it I see how wide the circle of people who were affected by his suicide really is. I'm sure that everything I have done, and do to this day, is affected by his death, and the way in which he died.

DEATH WITH DIGNITY

I n recent years society has viewed suicide under certain circumstances, and at least in some cases, as more legitimate and acceptable. This is particularly true in cases where the reason for the suicide is terminal illness or severe disability, when the person believes this will be a release from long term suffering and misery. In this case quality of life takes preference over life itself. In her bestseller *Me before You*[66] Jojo Moyes deals with attitudes towards suicide. In her book, the main character, who is totally handicapped after a car accident, plans to go to the Swiss establishment Dignitas.[67] "You can't let him do it, mother. You must stop him! It is not our choice, honey... I told him it's OK. Of course I told him so. What else could I do?"

Albert Cain refers to this form of suicide as altruistic. Using Durkheim's terminology he explains that this is why society tends to accept some suicides over others, adding that this is an ancient phenomenon. While society is organized and prepared to care for the elderly and the sick, there are those who commit suicide because they believe, rightly or wrongly, that by continuing to live they are a burden on others. Many families live with the knowledge that someone in the family feels this way and advocates this form of suicide, thus ultimately, the suicide does remove this burden from the family. Cain notes that in some cases suicide is carried out in order to release the individual himself, and not others, from the burden, in order to avoid what he or she considers a 'fate worse than death'.

It is not uncommon to read in the newspapers about elderly couples committing suicide, or grandparents taking the life of severely-ill grandchildren, and then committing suicide. An Israeli war hero, Brigadier

---

66 JoJo Moyes, *Me Before You* (2012)Pamela Dorman Books. Hebrew: Yeditoth Ahronot – Miskal, (2014) translated by Dafna Benowitz. P. 120,128

67 "DIGNITAS advocates, educates and supports for improving care and choice in life and at life's end." www.dignitas.ch. Retrieved 24.8.2015.

General Mota Gur's suicide, after years of suffering from cancer, was described as a "brave and noble act" by his friends. At Mota Gur's funeral former Israeli Prime Minister and President, Shimon Peres, said that he was determined to be true to himself, never compromising; this is how he lived, and this is how he died.

What makes me wonder is why a person who ends his life following unbearable *physical* pain is considered a hero, and yet people (and their survivors) who end their lives following unbearable *mental* pain, are stained and stigmatized.

'Death with Dignity' is what I consider to be equal to the phenomena of euthanasia, which legitimizes and actually allows persons to shorten their life when for instance they know they are terminally ill, thereby shortening their suffering. Accordingly, Death with Dignity takes place when people, usually old or sick, decide to take their own lives in order not to be a burden on their family or on society as a whole. Society generally considers this to be a heroic, rather than a selfish act. Prof. Israel Orbach claimed that in some suicides of elderly couples, the dominant spouse takes the passive one with him or her.

What happens to the suicide survivors, when the suicide is perceived as 'legitimate'? Are its implications on the survivors different? Amongst them, would we find the same reactions to their relative's suicide?

Michelle's father committed suicide after being confined by dialysis for many years. He was convinced that his condition would only worsen. In her story she sees her father, and his act, as heroic. On the other hand Sheila, whose elderly parents committed suicide together, expresses an ambivalent approach toward their act.

Paradoxically it seems that when the suicide is considered to be a heroic and altruistic one, there is even *less* space and legitimacy for the survivors to share their feelings, questions, anger, and loss. Even in cases where suicide is perceived as a brave act, deserving of respect and admiration, this may leave the family and relatives with feelings of neglect and rejection. Mark, whose sister committed suicide at the age of 16, refers to suicide as an active death, in which one continues arguing with the dead even years aft

Michelle

Let me begin by emphasizing that this is not the usual story one hears about suicide. From the little I've heard from people whose relatives committed suicide – some are angry, some could not accept the deed... in our case it was not like that. My father suffered from health problems and three times a week, for thirteen years, I drove him to the hospital for dialysis... for thirteen years. He was brave and he took responsibility for his life. He wrote letters in which he stated, "I do not want to be a burden to any of you. I just can't live like this anymore."

We all knew it was going to happen. We knew everything except the date. It was a suicide for bad-health reasons. The choice was to die after surgery or to commit suicide before. For him it was a clear choice. In fact, we understood and supported his decision, and we were prepared for it. My mother even said to him, "Your life is yours to live; your gun is yours to do with as you wish, once you decide that you can no longer cope - I won't stop you." I used to dress him, drive him to his dialysis, and on the way he used to say, "One day I'll shoot myself." There wasn't even an element of surprise. We got used to the idea, but if strangers had heard him speak like this they would have frozen on the spot. One day, he was told that his surgery was scheduled to be on the following Wednesday. He asked to be allowed to leave the hospital and go home the day before the operation. Meanwhile he parted from his friends. Throughout the day, every time I come into the ward they were all crying. When we came home he said, "Go to sleep, you're tired." And in fact I did doze off. At two-thirty in the morning he said goodbye to my mother, and went out into the fields.

A year earlier, when he talked about suicide, he said he planned to shoot himself in the living room. I advised him not to do it at home. I said, "Mom will never be able to go there after that." So he went away from the house.

His suicide made me really admire him. It was sad, but everything before that was sad. We admired him even more because he committed suicide. He became an idol. For me his suicide meant the end of his suffering. Of course we don't talk about his suicide with a smile on our faces, although... I know it sounds strange, but that's how I feel.

Other people have committed suicide, and people resent it and are angry with them... for years. How could they do it? And yet we feel that in our case it took courage to do it, we're proud of him! But I don't go around saying "My dad committed suicide." If I say that, people would get angry. Maybe it's not nice to say this, but I believe that death freed him. We knew that it would happen, and when it did we acknowledged that he succeeded, he did what he said he would. It wasn't even like having cancer. With cancer there is the chance of a cure, the chance of recovery; here it was just a matter of time. It was more terminal than terminal. I think that it's not even a bad scenario. It's not a good scenario, but on the last day when he knew that his suffering was coming to an end, he ordered two cheese cakes, and shared them out with everyone in the dialysis ward of the hospital. Later on of course I understood why. Everyone who knew him was not surprised by what he did. It was sad, but we weren't shocked. The other dialysis patients are angry with him. They are in the same situation as he was, but they know that they won't have the guts to do what he did. They asked me not to come there anymore and I was really offended. Why are they angry with me? What did I do?

When my father decided to end his life, my brother who lives abroad came to visit, but my father asked him to go back home. If my brother had stayed he would not have 'allowed' my father to do it. At one point my mother said to my father "Give the doctors a chance, maybe they'll succeed." But I told him that I have no problem with his decision. My brother is still angry, to this day. He really misses my father. Until it happened to us, I thought that suicide was one of the worst things that could happen, that it was absolutely terrible, that it was traumatic, something dark, like in the movies. To this day there are people who won't come to our house because they are afraid to say the word 'suicide'. Whenever I speak of him it brings a smile to my face. He was ill, and he suffered. And then he ended his suffering.

Whenever I potter in the garden it's as if I can feel him standing behind me telling me, "Not like that..." I really do talk about him with a smile on my face. He's like a living legend. What's really lovely is that, for me, he will always be a good father. Whenever I hear of an elderly couple who committed suicide together, I think that their kids are probably angry, but I think that if that's what the couple wants to do, 'good for them', especially if it doesn't come as a shock to the survivors. It's not like someone who got into financial difficulties and shot themselves. In that situation I would be angry too. What good comes out of a suicide like that? Do any problems get solved? But my father tied up all loose ends; he left letters for everyone... he even left a letter for the police letting them know that he had a license for the gun, and that no one else was involved. He wrote to his friends in dialysis, "I know that you'll be angry with me, but I sincerely hope that you don't get to the stage I am at, or feel as bad as I do." He left no stone unturned when it came to his friends and each one of his children. The end came, after thirteen years of preparation which began from the first day that he got sick. But the real loss and sadness felt by his death only sank in after about six months. Very gradually feelings of grief and loss swept over us. Each one of us experienced a different reality. If you'd interview my brother you'd hear a different story from mine. For me, it was planned to the very last detail; everything went according to plan, organized, and at the right pace.

I think that if my father had died on the operating table it would have been worse. He made it easier for us. He made us proud and confident to meet and deal with the people who came to our home to comfort us after the funeral. If it were up to him he would not want us to weep at the memorial services for him. That's why I collected all the stories about him, printed them out, and we sat and reminisced for hours. At some point we all began to sing songs from one of his favorite groups, the Gevatron, old Russian songs, and when people got up to leave the memorial service they shook our hands and said, "I know it sounds bad to say this, but I enjoyed this so much." My brother, on the other hand, found the memorial service problematic. I don't think he knew how much our father hated cemeteries and memorial services.

I think about death a lot. Whenever I have a muscle cramp I think that maybe I'm having a heart-attack. But death doesn't frighten me. It's something natural. That's life! All living things must die sometime. However my siblings won't agree to be interviewed by you. Men are different, they are afraid of showing their feelings or, God forbid, crying. When we were preparing for a memorial service, my brother said he would go and get the chairs, anything so he wouldn't be in or around the house.

Some parents don't take their children to the cemetery because they think it might be traumatic for them. I think that when adults take pity on children and don't tell them the truth, this is what harms the kids. I believe that the manifestation of trauma can occur after a number of years. There are some people who don't want to know, but for those who do, withholding the truth is harmful.

When people came to our house during the 'Shiva' my mother was the one who comforted them, and they left with smiles on their faces. I think that this is because she has so much 'common sense', she is so wise. I told her that I didn't grow up in her shadow; "I'm an apple that fell next to the tree." She says she is grieving and she wants to be allowed to mourn. Otherwise the grief will never be resolved and will lie buried within for years. She told us she believes that if people do not allow themselves to mourn properly it is harmful in the long run.

Sheila

I'll begin by giving you some background. In fact telling this story actually affects the experience itself. I don't call what my parents did 'Suicide' – I say that they took fate into their own hands, and this is not just a matter of semantics. They left a lot of written material behind. I feel as if they are with me all the time. I would go as far as to say that I talk to my father, I ask my mother for advice, even though some people think I'm crazy. I see that people raise their eyebrows so I tell them that I don't believe in the occult or things like that, but my parents are with me, and so are all the things they gave me throughout their lives. My mother was eighty three and my father was eighty four. My father was an artist who both painted and sculpted. I was always very busy working hard, but whenever I came home it awakened my own creativity. Sometimes I even hesitatingly pointed out little things here and there, little alterations for some of the sculptures my father created. I asked him if he minded me 'ruining' his sculptures but he always said "Go for it, it's my dream for you to do this too. After all, I believe that there's a little bit of God in everyone."

My parents took fate into their own hands. My father was the more dominant of the two. He was a planner. He believed that the taboo needed to be removed from the subject of death, and one should also plan for death. He said, "We planned the birth of our children, we planned our whole lives, we did everything according to plan; we will also plan our deaths." From about eighty years of age he spent more and more time planning and thinking about doing it. Of course everyone asks me if they were ill. On the contrary, my mother was a woman who loved life... they were both healthy. But this is how they planned to end their lives. Today I am sixty one years old. In this whole story each one of us, me and my siblings, has their own position. The last act in this story is integral to the story.

As I said, my parents decided to take fate into their own hands, the only question was when. My mother was less ready for this step. She was more vibrant, vital; my father after about eighty began to drop hints, little by little, that this is what they planned to do and that they had all the means needed to do it. Planning it took a few years. Some people think that you decide today, and tomorrow you do it, but it doesn't work that way. For ten years they planned how they would do it. There wasn't an article on the subject that they didn't read and they even asked me what I thought of the idea. In retrospect, I respect them for their decision. Occasionally I would drive them to visit my mother's brother in an old-aged nursing home, and when we'd leave my father would always say "Well, honestly, what do you think, is this a life?!" The nursing home was in the Carmel Mountains, and I would answer him each time, "Look at the great view of the sea!" This is always how our conversation would end. Usually I didn't like to get into this kind of conversation with them, but I knew what they were planning. I didn't like to talk about it though. I knew it would probably happen but I didn't know when.

When talking about life and death, emotions usually play a larger part than logic. My father was very rational and constantly dropped little hints. I was very close to my parents. In the last few years, after I suggested it, they moved to live near me. They had a house which they built themselves but said that they wanted to move to live near me while they were still independent. My mother said she wanted to be able to organize parties for the grandchildren. It's been three years since their deaths, and it's still hard for me to walk past their house, the house where they committed suicide. Obviously I don't want to go inside the house. Meanwhile, someone has already moved into it.

I know I'm jumping from topic to topic. I think about what they did all the time, day and night. We used to sit together in the evenings watching TV, and if my father would see elderly people, he would say, "What for, tell me, what for? Take all the money that's wasted on them and spend it on education. Isn't this a waste of money? These old people don't know where they are and who they are." This was the way he thought.

During what was to be their last week... they had planned the date a year earlier. They didn't change anything in their everyday lives, they lived according to their usual routine, but they had decided that after that date they would be no more. For a whole year they lived knowing the date upon which they had decided. But I didn't know a thing. How is it possible to live with that kind of secret? On a rational level, I understood and accepted that they would commit suicide; I even justified their decision. They left behind such a lovely warm home... their house was neat and clean, and they lay down like two angels. They looked so at peace and this helped me to come to terms with their act. They even left a note for me on the door which said, "We did it. Sheila, we did it, don't come in alone." Parting from someone is saying goodbye, but saying goodbye to both of them was a terrible blow. That was really hard. But I'm at peace with it. I respected everything they said, everything they did. Why wouldn't I? They left a letter in which they asked that if, God forbid, their plans didn't work out immediately, they begged not to be taken to the hospital. At that moment I said to myself that I would have lain down in front of the ambulance if one came to take them to hospital. I am telling you this so you can see how really at peace I was with what they did and what their requests were. Those were my thoughts and feelings at the time. But to say what would have been if... no-one knows. They also decided that neither one of them would leave the other to live alone. They did emphasize the whole time that this is not for young people. "God forbid, we are definitely not setting an example for others."

The topic of death by suicide touches many people, but the topic of death affects everyone. Sometimes I do say to myself "If they had lived another year, so it would have been one more year..." They were getting older, and dying is dying, and pain is pain. They are still part of my life. They wanted us to remember them as being strong, healthy and with all of their faculties intact, before they inevitably deteriorated physically. Understanding the situation gives you strength, but it doesn't make it easier. My emotions and my logic are still in constant conflict. My children are angry; they are less understanding than we are. They keep telling us that we should have prevented my parents from going through with their plan. They are really angry. They feel that as grandchildren they have been deprived of something good and pleasurable. I insist that the memorial services be only a small part of the way in which we remember them, because this is exactly what they didn't want. They wanted to be part of a family gathering, a walk in nature. People who remember them do not need to have a memorial service. We remember them together, as a couple, as a family. That fits what our parents wanted...

However, in spite of everything, with all the understanding, the bottom line is that *life is valuable*. There are no two ways about it. You can't deal with this in any other way. There are just some things that are and you can't reduce them to the sum of their parts. Even though I try, I can't always justify what they did life is valuable.

In their last week they started to 'say goodbye'. We had a party and everyone there was reminiscing about things that had happened over the years. On the way home my mother couldn't stop crying. It was clear to me that I couldn't prevent them from carrying out their plans. But why not postpone? Why now? I think my mother was prepared to delay it. In a sense, of course this meant not going through with the planned suicide. My mother was very optimistic.

I actually believe that when you take this step, it is always done too early. This was the problem. After all, they were both healthy. Once when my mother returned from a trip and she was struggling with her luggage I went up to help her, and she said, "When I need you to help me with my luggage, I won't be here anymore." But she was a lively vivacious woman, and was quite prepared to postpone their suicide. They talked about it, but my father was the one who really wanted to go ahead and do it. She wasn't quite as prepared as he was – I'm not saying that she didn't want to do it, she just wasn't quite as ready.

Even when you choose to die, death still remains a mystery. There is still a taboo surrounding the topic of death. It's mysterious because there's still the line between 'being' and 'not being'. I don't really understand what a person who decides to commit suicide thinks about. Perhaps they think only of themselves. My parents though, did think about others. They didn't want to become a burden on anyone. But no matter what, it does affect the rest of the family. I'm sure you (*to the interviewer*) are really angry. It's hard to understand, really hard to understand... I know that I say one thing and then I say the opposite, but in a way that's what life and death are. My father always said that death is part of life, and he said, just as he controlled his life, in the same way he wanted to be in control of his death. I once read a lovely description that education is like a valuable trophy that parents give to their children, and the children pass it onto their children, but not so that it will come back to the parents. Our parents didn't give us a trophy so that we could give it back to them. People tell us "Look what they saved you from." It's true but only to a certain extent. True and not true. We fluctuate between both sides of the argument. Wisdom in life is knowing when enough is enough. If you give too much, or too little, it's no good. At this point, the topic of euthanasia (Death with Dignity) comes in. If euthanasia was legal I have no doubt that we would have had them with us for a few more years. If you ask me what I would do, I don't think I'd have the strength to do what they did. There was a stage when I couldn't look at elderly people. If I saw an old healthy person I would say, my parents also could have been like that. And if I saw an old sick person, I would say "What good is this..." I still struggle within myself about whether it was right to respect that fact that my father didn't want to live. People can't really grasp what it means to die. I don't think it's possible to understand what it's like to 'be' and then 'not be'. Until someone comes back from the dead, we'll never know what's on the other side. It's impossible to apply logic to things that defy logic. There are people who go through really tough times, yet in spite of their problems, they fight to live each and every day they have left, to the fullest. The will to live is much stronger than the desire for self-destruction. When talking about the major issues of life and death, quality of life is a small detail. I wouldn't have the courage, or the physical strength, to do it. Then there's always the question of whether it's courage or fear. It's probably a combination of both.

I know many holocaust survivors who wouldn't talk about their experiences during the war. Only many many years later did they begin talking about those years. I don't think people like to talk about anything associated with death. When someone doesn't die of natural causes, there is even less discussion, even though silence is often more damaging.

Although ostensibly I have come to terms with their act, I also have very conflicting feelings. I must say that you helped me delve much more deeply than I dared to until now.

I want to go and visit their grave.

* * * * *

We go to the cemetery. Their grave stands out because it is so well cared for and there are many sculptures surrounding it. Even their letter box which was brought here from their home and symbolizes the line between 'being here' and 'not being here', something which Sheila talked about in her interview, is full. As we are leaving the cemetery she says to me: "This is the end of the story... actually maybe the end is the beginning."

* * * * *

In my mind, Sheila's story is, in some aspects, a mirror image to Michelle's story. Precisely because her parents chose to die while they were healthy, is Sheila able face the dilemma that exists in the conflict between preserving quality of life and the very fact of clinging to life itself. Wherever Michelle used an exclamation mark, Sheila placed a question mark. In fact we are talking about free will, and personal choice which leads to the line of thinking where people who choose the way they live their lives, should also be allowed to choose the way they die. Sheila spent a significant amount of time and energy analyzing this question over and over, and at the end of the interview she still was left with many unanswered questions. One answer, perhaps, to the question of why her parents chose to commit suicide, can be found in her father's view of life that "surely in everyone there's a little bit of God."

EPILOGUE

While writing this book and during the research which laid the foundation for it, I met many people – friends, relatives including children, parents, spouses, and siblings, of people who committed suicide. I always started the conversations by identifying myself as a researcher, an interested listener, and a member of the survivor community. From their stories, I learnt that suicide in a family is not a single story, with predictable implications and impacts. Rather, it is a collective experience with a diversity of narratives, an event which occurred under varying conditions and circumstances, impacting in different ways on the survivors. We cried and laughed together, shared what had happened to us since then, and talked about the impact that the suicide had on our lives. A warm hug at the end of the interview was taken for granted by people who had only met for the first time a few hours earlier. Each time we hugged, it stirred the memory of Susan's words: "I wanted to meet you in order to know that I am not alone," and Limor's words that we were "partners in the sisterhood of pain." We are not alone. Families who have had a relative commit suicide are exposed to an experience which has implications that are at the same time frightening and incomprehensible, yet have the potential to reinforce, strengthen, and shape one's character and the course of their lifetime. There is a partial answer to the question of what impact the suicide has on the family. This may be found in the Nobel Prize winner, Nadine Gordimer's words, quoted earlier in this book. She said people are divided into two groups, those who blame everything on their deprived childhood, and those who move forward and do not look back. The meetings and conversations with suicide survivors taught me that there is a third group: those who do look back, recognize the furrows that the suicide has plowed into their souls, and yet are able to move forward, adopting, accepting, and embracing these difficulties for what they are.

Suicide in the family is like a stone thrown into a well: the circles of the impact spread, and are far-reaching. Many family members, relatives and friends, will in one way or another, live in its shadow for the rest of their lives.

Although I heard many extremely emotional and disturbing stories on my journey to discovering the meaning of suicide for other survivors, and for myself, the bottom line of this journey was optimism. A suicide in the family is, as Susan put it, an aggressive act, causing a trauma which will last many years and its impact will always be felt. At the same time however, it may be a new beginning for the surviving family members. Many of us were raised with the idea of not sharing the difficulties in our lives, thinking that if we don't talk about our problems they would disappear. But problems live in our souls, waiting, in some cases for decades, until a chink appears, and they begin to seep out. Like Sisyphus, suicide survivors are forced to push their burden ahead of them, up the hill of life; the greatest difficulty is that secrecy makes this burden invisible. Exposing the secret will enable them, in some cases for the first time in their lives, not only to separate properly from their relative, but at the same time to get to know his or her healthy and beautiful aspects. They may also come to understand the more complex aspects of their relative's personality, aspects which may have contributed to the decision to take their own life. Incorporating the deceased into the family story also means reconnecting roots which were severed by their exclusion from the family story.

The secret is like a web in which the families are ensnared. As Roz said, "What do we not talk about? Things we feel ashamed of; things we want to hide." As long as the family members hide the 'terrible secret', they are actually trapped with the suicide and with the taboo surrounding it. The ability to talk about the deceased means that one can let go and say goodbye. As long as we keep the deceased hidden, it is as if we are accomplices to their act of suicide. Only the ability to separate and move on, clearly demonstrates that we are not ashamed of what we didn't do, and this will enable us to say goodbye, leave our deceased relatives, and go on without them, even though the scars remain with us.

In 1997, Mark Zukerberg asked whether secrets can exist at all in a world where the era of privacy has ended. Secrets involve a protected space in which one may hide, or may share only with whom one chooses, those parts of a person's world one is not willing to share with the whole of society. This space has protective functions, just like defense mechanisms. Yet maybe for the first time in history, social networks enable a common multi-generational social space. This is not only a technical change, but actually a fundamental one. This change opens new avenues of communication, helping, sharing, assisting, and being assisted; and we must exploit it, in order to reduce the anguish and distress caused by suicide, thereby expanding the circles of listening, supporting, learning, and helping.

In Judaism there is a saying, "Whoever saves a single life, saves the entire universe."[68] After the Hebrew version of my book was published, I received many responses and many different reactions. Many more people came forth and shared their touching, painful, and empowering stories with me. All the responses which came through letters, phone calls, or people I met in person, meant so much to me. Among them, some of the most significant ones were people who told me, "I had seriously considered committing suicide myself, but reading your book made me realize what a disaster I would create for my family and friends; I changed my mind." I believe that it is essential to talk about suicide, in order to ease any hidden or unspoken pain, and possibly prevent the next suicide; and at the same time enable people in need in general, and survivors, to know that they are not alone.

King Solomon, who is believed to be the author of the Biblical Book of Ecclesiastes (Kohelet), wrote: "There is a time to be silent and a time to speak." [69]

We have been silent too long. Now it is our time to speak.

---

68 Maimonides, Mishne Torah
69 Ecclesiastes (Kohelet), chapter 3:7

ACKNOWLEDGMENTS

First and foremost, my most profound thanks go to the interviewees of this book, who openly and courageously shared their personal stories with me, related their experiences following the suicide of their family member.

I began my journey of suicide and suicide survivors research, with the professional and empathic assistance of the late Prof. Israel Orbach, who was my mentor. No words can express my gratitude for all I have learnd from him.

Prof. Allan Borowsky, who ultimately became a friend, was the supervisor of my thesis, and was the first to discover that it is the impact of suicide, I am looking for.

My initial research which led to this book received an assistance from the Francesca Miller Fund, to which I am grateful.

Prof. Albert Cain encouraged me to believe my findings bear universal value and worth worldwide publication.

I wish to thank Miriam Klein Sofer for editing and translating this book, and for the wise advice and thoughts she shared with me during our work together.

I dedicate this book to my siblings – Gil, Dani and Iris.

Last but not least, I wish to thank the most amazing and supportive family I am blessed with, my husband Gideon and my children Sharon, Yuval and Alon, who traveled with me along this painful, empowering and rewarding path of exploration. They are, and have always been, my own private support group.

Many years after I began my interest in the field of suicide and suicide survivors, I discovered a note my father had written before he committed suicide. In his note he expressed the wish, that someone in need of help could find an assistance and support; this was not available when he needed it so badly.

May this book promote the awareness to the phenomenon of suicide and play a role in suicide prevention, and as such, be the fulfillment of my father's wish.

BIBLIOGRAPHY

Adler, R. *In The Name Of All Pain.* Tel Aviv, Sifriyat Poalim, 1979.

Akunin, B. *The Writer and suicide.* The author wishes to thank the translator Yigal Liverant for permission to use his translation from Russian (unpublished).

Allen, B.G., Calhoun, L. G., Cann, A. & Tedeschi, R.G. (1993). The effect of cause of death on responses to the bereaved: suicide compared to accident and natural causes. *Omega: Journal of Death and Dying* (28) 39-48.

Alvarez, A. (2011). *The Savage God - a Study of Suicide.* New York and London: Norton & company.

Amery J. (2004) *Beyond Guilt and Atonement.* Tel Aviv, Am Oved. Translated by Yonatan Nirad.

Amery, J. (2004). *Torture* Tel Aviv: Am Oved, translated from German by Yonatan Nirad.

Apter, A. & Freudenstein I. (2001). *Youth on the brink: suicide and suicidal tendencies* Dionon: Tel Aviv.

Aristotle, (1973). *Nicomachean Ethics.* Tel Aviv: Schocken. Translated by Joseph G. Libes.

Avrami, S. (2009). The hierarchy of bereavement in Israel – war victims, terror victims and suicide survivors. In: L. Sher and A. Vilens (eds.). *Terror and Suicide.* NY: Nova Science Publishers.

Arthur, B. (1972). Parent suicide: a family affair. In: A. C. Cain (ed.). *Survivors of Suicide.* Illinois: Charles E. Thomas 256-260.

Boldt, M. (1983). Normative evaluation of suicide and death: A cross-generation study. *Omega* (13) 145-147.

Bolton, I. *My son, my son. A guide to healing after loss of suicide.* Atlanta: Bolton press.

Bowlby, J. (1985). *Attachment and Loss: Sadness and Depression.* London: Hogarth press.

Brent, D. A. & Melhem, N. (2008). Familial transition of suicidal behavior. *Psychiatric Clinics of North America* (31)2, 157-177.

Cain, A. C. (ed.). (1972). *Survivors of Suicide.* Illinois: Charles C. Thomas.

Cain, A. C. (2002). Children of suicide: The telling and the knowing. *Psychiatry* 65 (2) 124-136.

Cain, A.C. and LaFreniere, L. (2015). Peer interaction of parentally bereaved children and adolescents: a qualitative study. *Omega: Journal of Death and Dying* 72(2).

Calhoun, L. G. & Allen, B. G. (1991). Social reaction to the survivor of a suicide in the family: a review of the literature. *Omega* 23(2).

Camus, A., (1979) *The Myth of Sisyphus*, translation by Zvi Arad, Tel Aviv: Am Oved.

Cohn, H. (1978). Suicide in Jewish Legal and Tradition. In: H.Z. Winnik and L. Miller (eds.). *Aspects of Suicide in Modern Civilization.* Jerusalem: Jerusalem Academic Press.

De Saint-Exupéry, A. (1981) *The Little Prince.* Tel Aviv : Am Oved. Translated by Arieh Lerner.

Duncan, C. and Cacciatore, J. (2015). A systematic review of the peer reviewed literature of self-blame, guilt and shame. *Omega* 71(4).

Durkheim, E. (1951). *Suicide - A Study in Sociology.* Illinois: Free Press.

Encyclopedia Judaica. (1971). Jerusalem: Keter Publishers.

Ezzel, C. (2003). The neuroscience of suicide. *Scientific American.*

Feifel, H. (1987). Grief and Loss: A review. *Society and Welfare* (3) 203-209.

Fennig, S., Geva, K., Zalsman, G., Weizman, A., Fennig, S.

and Apter, A. (2005). Effect of gender on suicide attempters versus nonattempters in an adolescent inpatient unit. *Comparative psychiatry* 46(2) 90-97.

Frankl, V. (1981) *Man's search for Meaning*, translation by Haim Isaac, Tel Aviv: Dvir.

Freud, Z. (1988) The Ego and the Id (1988). In: I. Orbach (ed) *Children who don't want to live: understanding and treating the suicidal child*, San Francisco, Calif., London: Jossey-Bass.

Fuchs, S. (8.10.1993) *Why write poetry if you can write jingles*. Maariv Newspaper (weekend edition).

Gefen Y. (1999) *Lovely Lady*. Tel Aviv: Dvir Publishing.

Goethe (1980) *The Sorrows of Young Verther*. Tel Aviv: Sifriyat Poalim.

Granot, T. (2000) *Without You: the Impact of Loss and Mourning on Children and Youth* .Jerusalem: Publication of the Ministry of Defense.

Gross-Isseroff, R., Biegon, A., Voet, H. and Weizman, A. (1998). The suicide brain: A review of postmortem receptor/transporter binding studies. *Neuroscience and Behavioral Reviews* 22(5) 653-661.

Gur, B. (1998). *A Stone under a Stone*. Jerusalem: Keter.

Gutter, I. (2004). *Suicide amongst Adolescents and Familial Bereavement*. Jerusalem, Hebrew University.

Hawton, K., Sutton, L., Haw, C., Sinclair, J. and Harris, L. (2005). Suicide and attempted suicide in bipolar disorders: a systematic review of risk factors. *Journal of Clinical Psychiatry* 66(6) 693-704.

Jamison, K. R. (1999). *Night Falls Fast: Uunderstanding suicide*. New York: Knopf.

Israel Statistics Yearbook (2000) Jerusalem: Central Bureau of Statistics.

Israeli Federation of Newspapers (17.7.1995) *Friends tell about her death*. Maariv Newspaper.

Karpel, D. *Late lust*. Haaretz, 24.10.2003.

Kubler-Ross, E. (1969). *On Death and Dying*. London: Collier McMillan.

La Ferriere L. and Cain, A. C. (2015). Peer interaction of parentally bereaved children and adolescents: a qualitative study. *Omega* 72(2).

Mann, J. J., Bortinger, J., Oquendo, M., Curier, D., Li, S. and Brent, D. (2005). Family history of suicidal behavior and mood disorders in probands with mood disorders. *American Journal of Psychiatry*, 162, 1672-1679.

Mann, J.J., Currier, A., Stanley, B., Oquendo, M. A., Amsel, L. V. and Ellis S. P. (2005). Can biological tests assist prediction of suicide in mood disorders? *Journal of Neuropsychopharmacology* (21)1-10.

Maris, R. M. (1981). *Pathways to Suicide: A Survey of Self-Destructive Behaviors.* Baltimore: The Johns Hopkins University Press.

Maslin, B. (1996). *The Angry Marriage: Overcoming the Rage, Reclaiming the Love.* Skylight Press, New York.

Myers, E. (1991). *When Parents Die - A Guide for Adults.* USA: Penguin Books.

Moss, S. M., Resch, N. and Moss, S. N. (1997). The Role of Gender in Middle- Age Children Responses to Parent Death. *Omega* 35(1).

Moyes, J. (2012). *Me before You.* Pamela Dorman Books: Viking.

Navot, T. (1996). *Do not raise your hand.* Tel Aviv: Ministry of Defense publication.

Negev, A. (29.8.1997) *she was two steps closer to it than others.* Yehidot Achronot Newspaper.

Negev, A. (2001) *Private Lives.* Tel Aviv: Yediot Achronot. Chemed Books.

Orbach, I. (1987). *Children Who Don't Want To Live.* Ramat Gan, Bar Ilan University.

Orbach, I. (2000). *Pain Unbound* Jerusalem: Schoken.

Orbach, I. (2001). Epilogue. In: Al Alvarez: *The Savage God: a Study of Suicide.* Jerusalem: Carmel.

Oz, A. (2002) *A Tale of love and Darkness*, Jerusalem: Keter Publishing, Israel.

Plato (1997) *Plato's Writings*, Tel Aviv: Schoken Publishers. Translated by Joseph Libes.

Pritchard, C. (1996). *Suicide - The Ultimate Rejection? A Psycho-Social Study.* Buckingham: Open University Press.

Pynoos. R. S. and Spencer, E. (1986). Special Intervention Programs for Child witnesses to Violence. in: M. Lystad (ed.). *Violence in the Home: Interdisciplinary Perspectives.* New York: Bruhner 193-215.

Ravikovitch, D. (1981) A Hard Winter from *Hovering at a Low Altitude: The Collected Poetry of Dahlia Ravikovitch.*Tel Aviv: Am Oved.

Real, T., (1998) *I Don't Want to Talk About It: Overcoming the Secret Legacy of Male Depression.* Scribner; New York, NY.

Richman, J. (1978). Symbiosis, Empathy, Suicidal Behavior and the Family. *Suicide and Life Threatening Behavior,* 8(3)139-149.

Rosental, R. (2001). *Is Bereavement Dead?* Jerusalem: Keter.

Schindler, R. (1996). Mourning and Bereavement among Jewish Religious families: A Time for Reflection and Recovery. *Omega* 33(2).

Shneidman, E. S. (1969). *On the Nature of Suicide.* San Francisco: Jossey-Boss.

Shneidman, E. S. (1982). *Voice of Death.* New York: Harper and Row.

Shneidman, E. S. (1986). Some essentials of suicide and some implications for Response. In A. Roy and B. Sher (eds.). *Suicide.* Baltimore: Williams and Wilkins.

Shochter, S. (1996). Loss of the Spouse. In W.C. Nihols. *Treating People in Families.* New York: Guilford Press.

Shtein, N., Chaklai, T., Aburaba, M. (2005). *Bereavement in Israel.* Jerusalem: Ministry of Health.

Solomon, A. (2001). *The Noonday Demon: An Anatomy of Depression.* Simon & Schuster, New York, NY.

Sonneck, G. and Wagner, R. (1996). Suicide and Burnout of Physicians. *Omega: Journal of Death and Dying,* 33(3) 255-263.

Stroebe, M. (2015).Is grief a disease: Why Engel posed the Question? *Omega* 71(3).

Suicidality and Data Collection – Workshop Summary, (2010). Washington DC: National Academic Press.

Tigenboren, E. (2001). I am a genetic Autonomy. Yedioth Aharonoth – Shiva Yamim Daily publication, Israel (16.3.2001).

Turov N. (1955). *The Problems of Suicide: A Psychological and Sociological Study.* Tel Aviv: Dvir.

Van Gogh, V., (2009) Letters to Anton von Raffard. In: (eds) Leo Jansen Hans Luijten and Nienke Bakker, *Vincent Van Gogh: the Letters,* US,UK, etc: Thames and Hudson.

Wertheimer, A. (1991). *A Special Scar: The Experience of People Bereaved by Suicide.* New York: Routledge.

Wickersham, J. (2011) *The Suicide Index: Putting my Father's Death in Order.* Tel Aviv: Ahuzat Bayit, Translated by Dana Elazar-Halevi.

Wrobleski, A. and McIntosh, J.L. (1987). Problems of suicide Survivors: A Survey Report. *Israel Journal of Psychiatry and Related Sciences* 24,137-142.

Zsalsman, G., Netanel, R., Fischel, T., Freudenstein, O., Landu, F., Orbach, I., Weizman, A., Pfeffer, C.R. and Apter, A. (2000). Human figure drawings in the evaluation of severe adolescent suicidal behavior. *Journal of the American Academy of Child & Adolescent Psychiatry* 39(8)1024-1031.

Yadin, Y. (1966) *Masada.* Tel Aviv and Haifa: Maariv and Shikmona.

Zalsman, G., Frisch, Apter, A. and Weizman, A. (2002). Genetics of suicidal behavior: candidate association genetic approach. *Israel Journal of Psychiatry and Related Sciences* 39(4) 252-261.

Zalsman, G. Frisch, A., Baruch-Movshovits, R., Sher, L., Michaelovsky, E., King, R.A., Fischel, T., Hermesh, H., Goldberg, P., Gorlyn, M., Misgav, S., Apter, A., Tyano, S. and Weizman, A. (2005). Family-based association study of 5-HT (2A) receptor T102C polymorphism and suicidal behavior in Ashkenazi inpatient adolescents. *International Journal of Adolescent Medicine and Health* 17 (3) 231-238.